JAM TREE GULLY

ALSO BY JOHN KINSELLA

Poems

Divine Comedy: Journeys
  Through a Regional Geography

Shades of the Sublime &
  Beautiful

The New Arcadia

Doppler Effect

Peripheral Light

The Hierarchy of Sheep

Zone

Visitants

The Benefaction

The Hunt

Poems 1980–1994

Graphology

Lightning Tree

The Undertow

The Radnoti Poems

The Silo: A Pastoral Symphony

Erratum / Frame(d)

Syzygy

Full Fathom Five

Eschatologies

Night Parrots

Fiction

Grappling Eros

Genre

Conspiracies (with Tracy Ryan)

Morpheus

Post-Colonial

In the Shade of the Shady Tree

Drama

Divination: Four Plays

Comus: A Dialogic Masque

Autobiography

Auto

Nonfiction

Disclosed Poetics: Beyond
  Landscape and Lyricisim

Contrary Rhetoric

Activist Poetics: Anarchy in the
  Avon Valley

JAM TREE GULLY

GULLY

POEMS

John Kinsella

W. W. NORTON & COMPANY

New York · London

For information about permission to reproduce
selections from this book, write to Permissions,
W. W. Norton & Company, Inc.,
500 Fifth Avenue, New York, NY 10110

For information about special discounts for bulk
purchases, please contact W. W. Norton Special Sales at
specialsales@wwnorton.com or 800-233-4830

Manufacturing by Courier Westford
Book design by Jo Anne Metsch
Production manager: Louise Mattarelliano

Library of Congress Cataloging-in-Publication Data

Kinsella, John, 1963–
Jam Tree Gully : poems / John Kinsella. — 1st ed.
    p. cm.
ISBN 978-0-393-34140-9 (pbk.)
I. Title.
PR9619.3.K55J36 2012
821'.914—dc22
                                        2011024795

W. W. Norton & Company, Inc.
500 Fifth Avenue, New York, N.Y. 10110
www.wwnorton.com

W. W. Norton & Company Ltd.
Castle House, 75/76 Wells Street, London W1T 3QT

1 2 3 4 5 6 7 8 9 0

for Tracy and Tim who live here,

for John and Mum who helped build the place

The author wishes to acknowledge

the traditional owners of the land he writes.

Chronology

Acknowledgements

The Adelaide Review; *Agni*; *Australian Literary Compendium*; *The Australian's Literary Review*; *Boulevard*; *Colorado Review*; *Eureka Street*; *Famous Reporter*; *Five Points*; *The Hampden-Sydney Poetry Review*; *Harold Bloom: 80* (Yale University Press, 2010); *The Iowa Review*; *Island Magazine*; *Manhattan Review*; *Meanjin*; *Or, Poetry*; *The New Republic*; *New Welsh Review*; *The New Yorker*; *Overland*; *Poetry Wales*; *Raritan*; *The Reader*; *Sha'ar—Poets and Poems 2010: The Ten Commandments* (Helicon); *The Sydney Morning Herald*; *The Times Literary Supplement*; *TriQuarterly*; *Warwick Review*; *Washington Square*; *The West Australian*; *The Wolf*; *The Yale Review*. And with thanks to my editor Jill Bialosky, and to Peter Pierce, Marjorie Perloff, and Susan Stewart for feedback during the writing of this work. I also wish to thank the University of Western Australia, where I am a Professional Reseach Fellow. And, of course, to Tracy Ryan.

JAM TREE GULLY

Prologues

LEAVE-TAKING (YORK)

Sprung, the wild-oat seed cocks
a grasshopper leg, and another
corkscrews into a heavy sock,
too thick for summer.

Sun skinks are fat on the fence
and a Christmas spider—horned
and enamelled—puts on a different face
to each approach—none is scorned

for its interest. No tree trunk
is straight and wasps coalesce
along the bricks, having sunk
larvae into huntsman spiders

and sealed their chambers that are a cross
between an oyster and charcoal colour—
mud that looks like the gloss
of pavers after too long in the fire.

Broadly speaking, I expect
things to look the same for some time
after we've left, lest it correct
where paths have worn and the climb

of plants that will make a winter
covenant prior to growth—the pattern
of germination, the plans, the failures:
each feat resolving expectations.

Today I saw the smallest monitor
stand off-centre and without fear,
studying me, its dugout a bold but gentle
opening, a valediction to unsettle.

THE LAND BETWEEN HOUSES:
FROM YORK TO JAM TREE GULLY

Wandoo woodlands
aren't haunted when knocked
down and hollowed
to the pit of their stomachs, burned

and cooked as good for nothing,
just ghosts on hallowed ground,
gravel guts we make roads from—strung
around the district while commerce resounds.

Arrival: First Lines Typed at Jam Tree Gully

To hold the walls of valley
downthrust limbs of York gum
liminality, flakes of granite
and lichen scored as sun inland,
glitterati, this Toodyay stone
broken where the building
has opened precipice,
erodability, that movement
where we walk, dislocating
weight of conversation, even
meditation, to contravene
our visibility, perched
up on high, sidereal.

A drawing out, the day
lessens, rampage
of dead and living trees,
entire collapsed structures,
signs of fire as jam-tree bark
blackened crumbles with touch,
all working shadows thin
up the hill, *the hill*. Kangaroos
stir from their shady places—
the heat so intense at midday
they don't do more than lift
their head as you approach.

In the dirt, laterite smudgings,
hard-baked patches of sand, coarse-
grained breakdown of quartzite
in its granoblastic glory, a sheen
of mica and feldspar configuring

a sandstone past, a declaration
of origins; what grows in what
was here before? It demands
reconnection or the hill
will despoil to its granite
core and nothing more,
nothing more. Dazzling
anomaly of pyrites, breeze
sharpened with 'fool', 'fool' . . .
welcome here . . . don't cling
together, give us roots
to nest among, cling to.

Common bronzewings heavy across the blank
of an arena we will fill with trees: sandy
spectacle, where horses rounded
on their tails: I see them twitch.

Internal fences down and out. Fewer
divisions. To predict a fate, changes
sweeping over an old old place; ring-
neck parrot feathers no divination.
What has chiacked in place
of undergrowth?

Weebills are here! And mistletoe birds
have been where mistletoe fruits have prospered,
have seeded jam trees, where nectar-hungry
birds of many varieties test the hardy flowers
drooping in swatches from thin, straining necks;
the parasitic engenders its own chains of being.
I am not asking to be part of it. With time,
something will click, I have no idea what. No
second-guessing, despite the weight

of hexagrams, I Ching. What else
I might read. Weebills are here!

Horseshoes and sheep skulls strewn across the block,
rare new growth, so late and odd. Fire wardens
watching afraid of vegetation? They have their own
version of prehistory, their own version of growth.

The making of place as a dynamic of couplings,
as if love and trust are omens, odds in your favour.
The sun burns but also fringes the leaves.

We Spend Days in This House

We spend days in this house but not nights.
We have seen the early morning sunlight
infiltrate the eucalypts, sunset deflected
by acacias. We have sweltered at midday.
We have walked every acre intimately.
The kangaroos recognise us and linger.
We spend days in this house but not nights.

In the extreme heat of the day the house
shelters us from the worst of it: it is not cool
but it is cool enough. A shade that doesn't
quite add up. Rainwater is 'sweet' if let run
for a minute, pipes clasping the scalding
flow. But you can't waste water,
so the run-off is retained in a bucket.

We spend days in this house but not nights.
Watching the bronzewing pigeons, hearing
their heavy flight—a kerfuffle—I wonder
if owls would call out, strain our dreams
like a fence—bright, sharp, to be tripped over.
You can't know what it's like without night, sleep.
We spend days in this house but not nights.

De-fencing the Block

We're pulling the fences out
from inside the block and opening
the fenced zone to the kangaroos
on the reserve—they favour the sand
of the old horse arena, making hollows
to stretch out in under the peripheral shade.
The kangaroos follow the same patterns
even after the fences are removed—jamming
their bodies between granite boulders
and where the fenceline was, not yet risking
a spreading-out, a taking-hold of what is theirs.

Stephen and John convinced me to buy a pair
of Maun fencing pliers—almost a hundred bucks
but they'll cut through high tensile strands
with ease. Through galvanised Cyclone Wire.
Ringlock fence, star pickets at fairly
narrow spread because this is a hillside
and it's hard to keep the tension. Every
so often a join in the fence grippled together,
a logical place to stop and start again
but we move on past, wire-ties unravelled
from star pickets, and the mesh rolled
into cylinders of light and polygons.

It's bloody work—my hands are a mess.
It makes me sick of reading poems about fences.
Or thinking poems about fences. As I cut away
with the Maun pliers—the hardest steel from England—
I mutter under my breath and John asks
if I am composing a poem. He's got used
to my patterns over the years. I often ask

him technical questions about tools and practicalities . . .
Probably, probably, I mantra, unhappy with myself.
He has invented a device for rolling the top wire
and that's his poem—unthreading the strand,
whipping back through the eyelets of star pickets,
then tying off into tight coils for later use. But where?

The kangaroos are gathering. Stephen and John
pulled down the electric fencing last week—removing
wire, insulators, energiser. The fence inside the fence.
The kangaroos have worked this out; now they're
on the inside as well. Both sides at once. They are not
strange animals. Poems from Barron Field to D. H. Lawrence
have done them no justice. And which species?
Here, it's Western greys. There'll be local Nyungar
songs that make sense, speak to the kangaroos, warn
them, celebrate them. I am sure if sung as strange
it will not be a 'genuine strangeness', or a 'weird melancholy'
or a grotesque or ill-conceived hybrid creature.
I could fact-check, but this is of the moment.

I am hot and burnt and have been rolling ringlock fencing
and have just seen a large male roo and a smaller female roo
and a joey not long out of the pouch. There are no sheep
on this block now—they left weeks ago—though
bones and lumps of wool lie about. The neighbours
will ask who or what will keep the grass down?! I say,
kangaroos eat! Some shoot them for eating crops.
Work it out. A syllogism. Still, we must mind our Ps and Qs
and not insult those who would keep the roos out,
who bust a gut erecting fences you'll tear down.
But then, my script is like cut wire
flailing about—only dangerous as you
let it be, but dangerous, if briefly, nonetheless.

Goat

Goat gone feral comes in where the fence is open
comes in and makes hay and nips the tree seedlings
and climbs the granite and bleats, through its line-
through-the-bubble-of-a-spirit-level eyes it tracks
our progress and bleats again. Its Boer heritage
is scripted in its brown head, floppy basset hound ears,
and wind-tunnelled horns, curved back for swiftness.
Boer goats merged prosaically into the feral population
to increase carcass quality. To make wild meat. Purity
cult of culling made vastly more profitable. It's a narrative.
Goat has one hoof missing—just a stump where it kicks
and scratches its chin, back left leg hobbling, counter-
balanced on rocks. Clots of hair hang like extra legs
off its flanks. It is beast to those who'd make devil
out of it, conjure it as Pan in the frolicking growth
of the rural, an easer of their psyches when drink
and blood flow in their mouths. To us, it is *Goat*
who deserves to live and its 'wanton destruction'
the ranger cites as reason for shooting on sight
looks laughable as new houses go up, as dozers
push through the bush, as goats in their pens
bred for fibre and milk and meat nibble forage
down to the roots. Goat can live and we *don't know*
its whereabouts. It can live outside nationalist tropes.
Its hobble is powerful as it mounts the outcrop
and peers down the hill. Pathetic not to know
that it thinks as hard as we do, that it can loathe
and empathise. Goat tells me so. I am being literal.
It speaks to me and I am learning to hear it speak.
It knows where to find water when there's no water
to be found—it has learnt to read the land

in its own lifetime and will breed and pass its learning
on and on if it can. Goat comes down and watches
us over its shoulder, shits on the wall of the rainwater
tank—our lifeline—and hobbles off
to where it prays, where it makes art.

Dream of What's Below

Because it's temporary, while we build on rooms
for the family, we stretch out in the heat
on the sofa-bed. It's called an 'Albany',
though we're seven hours' drive away
from the coastal town, its namesake,
and the inland heat is devastating. We
try to recall sea breezes. I fan Tracy
with whatever comes to hand, then drift off
into a half-awake state—I can see my hand move,
the fan move, then I briefly dream . . . a breach in the fabric
of wakedness, heat, sleep, the fan, the sheet
over the Albany dampening with sweat . . .
I dream of what's below this stony place—
Coondle, the Ballardong people call it—
'stony place'. Loose stones and larger stones
and a solid dome of granite beneath.
A hundred and eighty feet down the bore
was drilled through rock and dirt, into
porous rock, into a freshwater stream.
I dream filtration and the passage
of water through sand, subterranean
sand, the tunnels and sheets of liquid.
I wake drowned in sweat, the fan
dropped by my side, and Tracy
sitting up, faint with heat.

Eagles at Sunset Stock Epithet

Climbing to the highest part of the granite
a trembling in the warm air of sunset—a literal
vibration of the wattle trees—a pair of wedge-tailed
eagles sweeps up from the restless valley,
to hover on degrading thermals—falling a little
then readjusting, an eye to the ground for evening
awakenings in shadows and clefts of granite,
the compensation. They semi-circle us,
then fall away downhill at an angle, as if
to cope with the gradient as *you* would walking
up the steep slippery slope. Gradient of air,
of uplift. We devise a hapax legomenon to cope
with the strangeness. Night falls and we climb
back down to the house, oversensitised—almost—
to the movements of what the eagles were after,
a transference we're not ready for—true or not,
wishful thinking, hunger for thermal imaging.

Reptile Life

A reptile book is a way of saying language
isn't tired in your hands, looking up a species.
Photo ID or running a finger down an index.
Eyes, skin, elision. What tongue twists its warning.
A book of riddles in that old between-the-epochs speech.

We measure life by their presence—snakes
and lizards. They ripple gloss across the pages,
exfoliate granite. Quiet in the biting sun.
But beneath a boulder, an easement cupping
a blue-tongue skink, the largest I've ever seen.

What do we say to that? Nothing in the pages
to correlate. Brandishing in the shade,
smoothed to cool and breathing slowly,
travesty of winter in mid-summer apostasy.
It watched with one eye and paced its heartbeat.

Without religion, we make our exegesis
out of amateur herpetology: those shiny
pages, measures of scale and thermoregulation.
Heating or cooling, we exclaim the wonder
of observation. It fits the picture and outgrows it.

An Elective of Gradients

You choose which inclines you show a friend,
or which inclines your friend might favour—
but he makes his own way through the stones
and up the steepest parts and is interested
in what happens when water runs and cuts.
He is interested in gradients and erosions,
in the pair of eagles that come at dusk
before shutting down, in the echidnas
eating the termites that hollow York gums
that 28 parrots nest in. He is interested
in bringing his boys up here to plant trees,
to labour. I offer to pay them and him
but he declines, saying he would like them
to labour where the steepness sharpens
seeing and their work will grow without end.

Hive Liberty

Most of the York gums here are old
and hollow. Many are dead and collapsed
open like a star losing its mass. Inside
one, down in the gully, bees have invested
an opening, a hollow where a limb has torn
away and termites have eaten the rings
of time. It echoes with bees, wild and intense
through the fissure, fanning flames
of neologisms because 'feral' doesn't fit.
It is not for a poem to explain why—
that would extract the figurative and ambiguous
and render the account too prose-like . . .
The bees encircle me as I look closely,
but unalarmed, and ready to move on; *that's it*—
I am stung but they remain calm and intact
and none die because of my presence.
I impose a reading of the 'tyranny
of the majority' on their actions,
but know the queen deep in the hollow
shifts the political ground, and ritual
and custom are consensus, and knee-jerk reaction
is what I have in both caution and anxiety.
I will show the rest of the family,
but warn them to go only *so* close—
not as close as I went: curious, arrogant,
sure I'd make it through and become
staunch defender of hive liberty,
co-existence wherein we title our claims.

Leak

The ninety-thousand-litre rainwater tank
is concrete and afflicted by cracks—where
water leaks through, lime and algae react
with water and air and seals the cracks.
At present, there is a large fracture
that won't close over, though layers
of plant and mineral are building.
Small birds—probably thornbills—
grip this formwork and drink
as if from a slowly dripping tap,
the trace of water in forty-degree heat
doubly enhanced by the shade. Pinpoint
beaks catch a droplet and tilt back
with a flash that would ignite all around,
so combustible, so traumatised
by dryness, the eradication of moisture.
The leakage is remarkably cool
as it emerges, so much pressure
behind it, concrete perspiring
in the volatile and oily air.

Sheep Leg

In following the waterway across the hill,
York gum saplings holding out against
the erosive sidewash induced by downpours,
you come across the leg of a sheep, flesh
eaten away, bones held together by sinews
that have dried and tightened—the leg
is seized in the moment of 'fall to your knees . . .'
It points neither up nor down the hill, nor divinely
the length of the waterway. A sheep death
under the old regime, a time when sheep
kept the grass down and died to rot
where they fell. Dismembered by foxes;
strewn about. Most of the corpses
were relocated before we arrived,
but the odd bleached skull, thigh bone,
clump of fat and wool remain. And the leg.
It keeps its own counsel.

Evening

Kangaroos find their way through and over
the fence as light burns the rim of valley
and dusk lifts up out of the gully;
a golden whistler calls late and melodically
but with a slight difference—a last singing—
from highest point of hillside
from highest branch of tallest York gum;
gunfire pocks distantly, as if it can't let go
before dinner, but the breakdown of light
is killing time, awakenings that most threaten
owners of weekender blocks, of farmlets,
most threaten retirees from large properties
who can't let go of old rituals, of killing times.
Some creatures pass by and don't return:
new ecologies new evolutions new ideas
of territory, and out there, control tampers
with mutual aid, anomaly not quite grasped
outside, tolerated as a curiosity
for the time being. We know places
kangaroos rest during day, gathering places of night,
dawn signings-off when knowledge inverts
REM sleep: the sign is invoker of dreams
and the full moon ranges free
through their chartings.

Saturday Afternoon

There is no lyric in gunshot,
no song in the spread, the grouping
of bullets puncturing the target
across the valley, down in its heart.
The *pop pop* goes against the wind,
against the rush back to pick up oxygen,
then the wind shifts and carries the *crack*
crack closer to us: you pretend you're alive,
like protest. There is no freedom.
Across the Shire boundaries
votes leak and old farming families
hold sway, knowing what's good for the place.
They subdivide and loathe the city ways
weekend residents bring with them;
in the same way they want to shoot *ferals*
when their not-so-far-back ancestors
brought ferals with their feral selves.
They deny any ownership prior
to their own. They sell a 'tree change'
to pay for the new tractor which knocks
down the trees. Ash and soot lift
in waves from the burnt paddocks:
wisps of aspiration and belonging,
a swirl of uneasiness and insurrection.
On a chunk of granite by the corner
of Jam Tree Gully, Tim saw a bearded
dragon and I didn't believe him!
But it was there, still and staring up
as a *crack* stretched across the gully
and it dashed off, the two moments
       possibly unrelated.

Solitude

The water doesn't pool here, but flows
past fast into the valley, down towards
the creek, the tributary, the Avon River.
A disrupted solitude, the washaway, as soil
is dislodged and we are diminished. Jets
from Bullsbrook run up the valley
on a deviated flight-route, training to keep
the valley intact, to ward off the rapacious?
Alone, it's too filled with prospect,
though I know birds are more active
just after daybreak. I make disobedience
by ignoring their flypast, their violence,
but something like weather gathers
in their wake, and the boom that might
follow the lean times of the living—
birds, animals, plants—keeps
its own counsel, not made or not
reaching us, as if a world apart,
off the glowing screen.

Away

Poet: See those clouds; how they hang!
— THOREAU, 'Brute Neighbors'

A return makes the away a filling-in.
The nano and vertices rarefy and offset
cardinal vowels: I count trees dead,
trees survived, an erosion through blown
sunlight, a rush of dryness down storm-cuts
in the hill. Away, I marked each day
with an itinerary, not times or species
but movements and interstices. I reworked
pronunciations knowing that even a couple
of weeks change everything, and that this change
had not gathered or had only formed ectopically
in my lymph nodes: this dialect I cart around
with me, that I take away and spread like offerings,
I say, 'Clouds hang over the valley, see how
the galah hangs in their wake, the eagle
tears at their display . . .' and some hate
the 'site' of them: the eagles and clouds,
and I can't understand whether I am here or away.

Reading

(1)

When scramble bikes have blazed
their way, they sign off with a flourish,
repetition showing there's nothing to be
discovered, just covered and re-opened.
Stroke of engines in long dry grass
spark a district and write it over—
kangaroos are crushed against fencelines,
limbs tangled. Two red-capped robins
glow into focus and read the York gum saplings,
too many saplings bunched together
to survive the long summer,
competing for the same water.
Reading is competing, a formal
innovation of roots and scant moisture
grabbed from early-morning air—or
reading the shattered concrete
where lightning traced a hairline fracture
across the rainwater tank, pre-articulation
or an end to language. The biosphere
keeps the particles of the dead
close to prayers, indifference, non-
belief. Atmosphere prevents
them being lost, escaping, diluting
in the vacuum, the slow gravitational
urge to find another planetary home.
And I believe this, reading the stars
for want of another text, denying
the astrological, enamoured of astronomy.

(11)

I speak to the ranger about the bikes
ripping up the reserve—he says fire
is non-negotiable and I say fire
puts us on the same page. Fire
is a dead end with no mystery.
Its rebirths are an 'as the case
might be'. The smudge of ghosts
parodies our dialogue as paddocks
smoulder with autumn dryness.

Extending the House at Jam Tree Gully

Extending the house on the hillside
to cater for more of us and our more
is a disturbance to the eagles who fly over
and the kangaroos who come across
from the reserve in the morning.
The space of building-into is already
flat and covered in gravel—beneath,
is clay and stone, a lot of stone.
No plants, no animals, will be
cleared to make way for the add-ons,
though even in hard ground things
live unseen by us. It is nothing
to do with nature, this act of living
of ours. This providing for family.
But we will look out new windows
down on the trees long there,
and the understorey we are filling in.
The making and the feeling
of goodness is another type
of nature again, and it won't resolve.

Digging

Ground baked so hard you can only scrape
and pick at it, occasionally shattering
into sheets and chips around a rocky protrusion.
It is dirt around stone. Prise and quarry.

The trees around the blank space you aim
to plant, say something about Rousseau
as you turn over states of nature,
the inherent goodness of anti-social
behaviours absurd in the heat. Filling gaps.

Digging in dryness with roots of a transplant
seedling singed like hair, though living hairs
and not the dead white hairs of your own head,
sweat-slicked under the hat, a failure to acclimatise,
catch the little moisture that comes with evening.

Digging against the grain of the hill, feet
slipping as you struggle to grip—mountaineer—
to reach finally deeper into the earth
than the length of the seedling's root system.

To breach a tunnel, a vein through which white ants
migrate to their next meal, next tree with a grey
dead heart, to take community lock stock and barrel,
damaged by air and light which you quickly
cover them against, though curious

to know if the queen might move through
that small aperture, or if she transmigrates.
Filling the digging in around the roots, tilted
away from the white ants' conduit, who might
just taste to see if the cellular intrusion

so nearby is living or dead, how the cellulose
might digest, pass through their body
back into the rocky soil. The dirt stays under
my fingernails. There's not enough water
     to clean it away.

Some Sounds at Jam Tree Gully

The wattle seed in its curled throw-out pod
    is the sound of ejection in the heat.
The codicil is collateral, and a hook
    is what collated the crops.
Among that 'deficiency of domestic sounds'
    we hear the croup of a waterbird
on the dry hillside. Its syntax is convoluted.
    If I quote, 'more indigenous
than the natives', I open a discourse
    on the wrongs of plain English,
an embarrassment of riches to the thieves
    of the district, their real estate
argot. Irony of the big breath—an easterly
    pushing the seeds out of range,
the waterbird's jargon into the friction of leaves.

Storm Cicadas

Cicadas ring loudest when you're alone.
Up on the hill you are so close to the thunderheads
you can almost touch them. Standing on boulders
you invite a lightning strike, but it's not from there
you notice that a storm is active within the storm,
that it has its own earth to strike up from,
to connect with. In there, night has already
collected and will drop like a black sheet,
to be ripped up then healed again. In there are
the mixed metaphors and split infinitives
you grew up fearing—your mother
an English teacher. Storm cicadas
halve the day. Birds make late flights,
late swoopings. They risk being closed out.
It's the ringing in their ears. Last week,
climbing a staircase down in the city,
you thought a young bloke descending
was going to slam your head into the wall,
and that would be it for you. Nothing.
He passed by awkwardly, benignly,
but you sensed that immensity of *nothing*.
The storm within the storm doesn't know it exists.
It sees nothing destroyed when it strikes.
It just strikes and things look the same
though you know in description things change,
rearrange, and roll further east. You keep dying
and filling the nothingness, the absolute silence,
with cicadas and birds, storms within storms.

Desire Lines

Down to the water-trough the sheep's desire
glows with wearing: a dead certainty, a shaved-
to-the-dust rendition. Each time I rename
the same veins, the same watery heart, same theory
as if it will absorb the emotion of the dry:
the bores draw and can't reach the water-table,
retreating or sucked too hard. The valley
is too wide for stimulus, too wide for white
goods—four-star energy ratings, digital
widescreen televisions. This is the cake of isolation:
the getting closer, subdividing, hoping for amenities,
utilities, a thriving trade in alpacas and olives.
Then there's us: disconnecting, replanting.
So, something's got to give. Desire lines
only thread one way, we are told, and the rule
of the majority sheers under the weight.

The Dry Dry

Trees that survive most long summers,
that survived years of flatlining drought,
are yellowing and moving towards dying-off.
The dry is drying out, and from the top
of the hill down, the top of trees down
are extinguishing. Around the great boulders
at the plimsoll line of the block, dirt edges
are moving away, creating space, a zone of slippage
and falling, taut with astringent moss, dead
as instruments of cutting—flakes of granite
splitting off—the dry place knows a new dry,
a dry we can't stop. A mob of roos moves
through and their eyes are the sand of glass
with no moisture—inside, a lens turns
nothing upside down, and dry makes waves.

Eagle Affirmation

You've got to understand that sighting the pair
of eagles over the block, right over our house,
not more than twenty feet above the roof,
so massive their wings pull at the corrugated
tin sheeting even with gentlest tilt, counteracts
bitterness against all the damage I see and hear
around me on an exclusively crisp blue morning,
when clarity is pain and even one small missing
wattle tree, entirely vanquished since I was last here
at home—I still find this hard to say—is agony;
a region is not a pinpoint and a different compass
works in my head, having magnetics for all
directions and all pointing to one spot
I know and observe as closely as possible;
and even one small vanished or vanquished
wattle tree is agony close to death for me,
where I find it hard to breathe to feed myself
to get past the loss; but the pair of eagles
still appearing and keeping their sharp
and scrupulous eyes honed, overrides
this ordeal, though I wish their victims
life too and their damage is traumatic
as anything else; that's as much sense
or nonsense as I can make in such blue light.

Single-lined Photos

The bullant joins shadow and light at the mouth of its volcanic
   pit.
The golden whistler settles in a half-branch that bends to its
   shape, its colour.
The shrike-thrush prises the bark apart to scrutinise a
   micro-climate.
Five brown-headed honeyeaters grip lime bubbles on curved
   concrete to taste water.
The female grey kangaroo approaches the fence as does its joey,
   unsexed.
Swaddled in leaves the weebill puffs up to twice its size, eyes small
   but intense.
The orb weaver strung neatly between trees overwhelms but a
   small red spot shines beneath and the dead and the waste it has
   made climb upwards.
The male orb weaver, part of the same picture, is small but indis-
   creet on her tail.
         The eagle off-centres and fills its beak with its head.

Lichen Glows in the Moonlight

Lichen glows in the moonlight
so fierce only cloud blocking
the moon brings relief. Then passed by,
recharged it leaps up off rocks

and suffocates—there is no route
through rocks without having to confront
its beseeching—*it* lights the way,
not the moon, and outdoes epithets

like phosphorescent, fluorescent, or florescent:
it smirks and smiles and lifts the corner
of its lips in hideous or blissful collusion,
and birds pipe an eternal dawn, never knowing

when to sleep or wake. They might
be tricked into thinking their time's up,
in the spectrum of lichen, its extra-gravital
persuasion, its crackling movement

remembered as still, indifferent, barely
living under the sun, or on a dark night;
climbing up you'd escape, but like all great
molecular weights it leaves traces

you carry with you into the realms
    of comfort and faith.

Kangaroos in the Fog

There is no difficulty having a conversation
with roos up on the stone of the hill—they
watch as intensely as being watched and define
what they will and won't tolerate clearly;
they are articulate in many languages.
They leap across the screen of the window,
cosine-ing the graph of the block, marking
time between York gums. The green tint lifts
between their leaps and day is limitless.
You can see just far enough in this hillside fog
if you know how to look. The strike of type-
writer keys is a percussive warning as all
writing is, no matter the good intent,
the plea to speak, the plea to be heard.

Balloon

It didn't happen in that order—
the endless growl of what will turn out to be
miniature quad and trailbikes, carried along
the top of the valley and rumbling its contents:
small kids with helmets weighing more than their heads,
ragged on by parents with crossed arms and ambition
in their eyes: round and round the drone of fun.
A country pursuit. Tracy tells me a professor
of economics at a local city university
while praising capitalism says he will only
listen to opposition if it comes from one
who eats only lentils, has given up cars
and eschews imported brands of foodstuffs. Lentils?
Contradictions aside, I'll take him on, though
it might be hard to hear me speak above the junior
quad-bike circus performing along the hills. But hark,
I'll tell you something unusually usual: at dusk
wandering the block with Katherine we came across
shreds of chemical-pink balloon with plastic string
attached to its tied-off umbilical cord, clearly
an escapee from a party, the child—her name
decorating the balloon with three crosses for kisses—
in tears, chasing it up into the sky, watching
it drift over the hills, her letter to the world
a single word and her mark made over. Katherine
asks if I recall the balloons her class back in England
released with school name and address and how one
floated all the way over the Channel and on to Belgium
where another child picked up the shreds and deciphered
the message and wrote back; weather balloons, 'hopes
and ambitions' as Delmore says, but without doubt
or scepticism, in full expectation they will land

somewhere far away and bring joy to the finder.
I dispose of the shred of balloon, fearing
an animal crossing the block in the dark,
night-eyed and keenly sampling the ground
and the air with its snout, will reread or misread
the code of chemical pinkness, and like some Red
Riding Hood in reverse, choke on the gift of chance.

Rehabilitation is its own profanity

The randomness of planting wattles on the hill
above the house has its own profanity—the shaping
of guesswork, or to plant where you stop thinking,
or to toss a stone up and follow its arc to plant
where it lands, nudging aside and then ringing
a sapling with *that* stone and others around.

Rehabilitation is its own profanity—who am I kidding?
Almost easier to take a place long ceased to be pristine
and make it better. The delusion of healing. It passes
a life, it pushes prime concerns to the back of the mind.
I've only seen one or two small birds while out and about
today—planting, nurturing. I lay plans for future

restoration, talk about the long-term. Shadows are thinner
and longer and that stone emits a changed, unsettling light.

This will not be a model farm

There is a new set of shelf fungus
on the overarching branch of York gum
by the lower rainwater tank—small tank
that once watered stock which are no longer
grazing the block—all that walks here now,
come and goes by other rules, even the lost
dog that was heard barking and left a shit
as it passed by. I won't introduce
new names but search out the old.
That's not appropriation—it's respect
and learning. Knowledge is the tree
replanted in the ashen bed of an old stump,
a partial mythology; I'd like to call it
'a Greek theatre', say, Epidavros
I visited as a young man,
but it doesn't work—verse
doesn't make model farms,
even when ground-out in perfect
meter, the reader drained, waiting
for substitution. I planted that sapling
in ash-soil with acoustics of the lost
tree resounding in ways we can't be sure of,
and in the now wet and malleable earth,
hidden rocks emerge easily and lay claim
to surface. See, this is neither model farm
nor churchyard, though a wounded
spot of ground is set aside for olives.

Bulbs and Corms at Jam Tree Gully

On the bare brow of bloody dirt
in front of the house we're learning
there are six seasons, that thick
green shoots of bulb-growth divide
winter. Beneath the 'randomness'
of native trees, they stand out
precisely. I'd guess freesias
and daffodils. In summer
and its adjacent seasons, the hump
of dried-off foliage was ambiguous.
You couldn't tell with confidence
that anything else would ever
emerge. But then, Cape tulip
is a 'weed' throughout the valley,
and not seeing it in summer
doesn't mean its orange-pink sea
of exclusion won't draw
the poisoners to try—failingly—
to wipe it out. What dormant intent's
contained in bulbs and corms
that people hate? What odes
to mystery and constrained sexuality
do they possess? Maybe more,
a warped self-hatred the freesias
and daffodils clench but don't name:
bold as brass on a spring morning,
never looking over their shoulders.

New Lichen!

Conditions are perfect—so perfect—a radiant
green lichen has established itself just off from the sunset
side of a jam tree. It blooms like a rose, body
upright and out there and curled to grasp, collect
what's going. Not domiciled acceptance, fringing out
on granite like a half-hearted echo, defeated shadow,
antidote to Narcissus. This newly established heart
of a colony is redolent, is lush and succulent, and draws
you in close like a Venus Flytrap—it truly looks carnivorous
and you know your end is written in curiosity. The real
estate agent would say you control the ground that wattle
grows out of and thus the lichen—that the landscape
'radiates from me accordingly'—but I don't believe
what I know can't be true. Lichen says so. I hear
it in fresh winter voice, lucid and numinous,
fully knowing the structure of its language.
Some say I eschew the facts, but facts live with lichen
on granite and not jam tree—related, and as determined
to make ends meet even when the sun has sucked
life out of surroundings, the strength of the old lichen-eye
is in the iris, and not the pupil. The brand new lichen
tells me this is not what it looks forward to—its host
an old jam tree that won't live much longer, that will rot
and powder away rapidly. And so the lichen increases
its brilliance, and I hear no object lesson to take away.

Inverse Brass Rubbings

The rain has come with remorseless indifference
to the absolutes of drought—'take that', I say it says.
It pools and complies and etches downhill—it runs
and collects like perfect science, the intricacy
of veinwork in any living body. The block is in relief.
Inverse brass rubbings that tell us art is always
a copy—the battered sky threatening to erase
work already done: granite chunks exposed,
sand spread out from the arena in deltas
and estuaries, the hacking cough of the plunge
down the steepest part of the hillside, red earth
lesions and the first step in making valleys.
I am going to plant saplings of eucalypts
along this gurgling airway, which will become
great trees holding back the deluge. Likely,
this year will be an aberration and the trend
to dryness thrust ahead, a dry tickle then a barking
dry cough. But I can see where water goes now
when it flows, and why the weaknesses
of land are all in the seeing and what's been
covered up to make the best of the way
we've made it, what we'd hope to undo.

The town and river overflow

The town and river overflow as competitors
prepare for the Avon Descent—canoeists
with their low-impact skills, and vandals
in their powerboats who wish to brutalise
the odds. Out here, far away really, at a point
where water runs off hills and collects
in the valley to feed a creek tributary that adds
to the rush of white water over rapids, stoking
the main event, you see none of them. It is so wet
the subsoil drain beneath the house is working
overtime, and gouge marks down the slope
are furious and undermine each other in their
against-the-quickest-descent pull. What gets
in the way of reaching the lowest point, to collate
flow and hydraulics of inland looking outwards,
ocean, or cloud which vaguely suggest
more rain, more fuel for white water racing
that brings people from places where there
are no banks to erode, no original vegetation
to prise from flimsy vantage points. Down
in town business is brisk, and the moment
is lived: only so many consequences
can undercut books, bank balances—
an audit of souls and bodies and where they fit,
taking the quick way out or passing town
fast in their race for a line so far downstream,
an end to which the town and river overflow.

Architecture without ornaments

In this simple house there are still dozens
of picture-hooks on the walls, so close together
we know the previous occupant needed crowded
images of family and horses. This was a horse place,
and we have pulled down all internal fences,
removed strands and insulators of the electric fence;
the evidence is everywhere. The great shed built
on a cut in the hill above the house is still
decked out as stables—stalls, false floor
of hay where bales were stacked, room for
grooming and medicating and hanging saddles,
straps, and tote bags. Bit by bit we'll undo, welcome
owls and carpet snakes into high places, redo
the floor. And though we add rooms to the house
for children and books, we disconnect slowly
from the outside world—an architecture
without ornaments, designed by us, built
by J.A. and tradesmen he calls on as need
arises. Keep it simple. Let it blend into what's here,
work its way back to roots, rockface, deep
streams that run beneath, but not as design
to mask comfort and trappings pretending
to be art, but just the necessary, basic necessities,
without semantics and points of view adapting
like interpretation, owl and python considering
the short movement downhill one worth
making, as the house, too, could almost belong.

Cloven Hoof

The sandy arena is strewn with footprints—cloven
hooves. There seems no point of entry and no point
of departure. There are fresh droppings, some loose
as if too much green stuff has been eaten too fast
after the long dry spell. It makes no sense. Wild goats?
Possibly . . . come out of the neighbouring reserve,
but I can't detect tracks or goat scats on that side
of the line. The plethora the multiplication the exponential
cloven hoof—with cloud-cover hugging the hills
it gets so dark, even too dark for just smell and touch
to find a way across. Which might account for the rush
of steps, the frantic ring around, haunting leap from
a distant space, that even bad press, propaganda, light
the piercing eyes of goats, so hunted down, devils in every
farmer's almanac, even those who profit from them.

Higher Laws

It's a month since we've been here
and dandelions have confirmed a rampant
occupation: in lieu of us, as vanguard,
eyes to the eyes of our boots. A grey
kangaroo and a wallaroo which we
haven't seen prior: *good,* brown and grey
species mixing in *style indirect libre,*
not mating but in the vicinity, this vicinity,
of 'distress', of sand flowing down
from the old arena, washed off
notational rewrite of boundaries,
or an old boundary we might tap into,
dark sky opening permission to latch onto,
our gross senses making appetite of vista,
close-up realisation that every tree
planted has been eaten down to roots,
and further, further down. So, celebrate
this feeding of hillside we are part of,
focalised characters that we are,
acting outside the kangaroos' court.

Spring Pollen

> Thus it seemed that this one hillside illustrated
> the principle of all the operations of Nature.
> The Maker of this earth but patented a leaf.
>
> —THOREAU, *Walden*, 'Spring'

Yellow overwhelms, satiates,
blocks out the picture of hillside: leaves
wave in mild suns, searching out
attention. This is not subjective

and would happen if I weren't there
to observe; screenprints of pollen,
dusted cuffs come out of black centres,
not yellow petals. Suffusion,

volatility, risk of drowsing off
when everything that can, will pounce
or crawl over you and either way
consume. We wade through senses

we can't name but know are there,
bothering blood. Grandparents
might say: we feel it in our waters,
our noses tingle before the flowering.

Holidaying on the coast, we invoke
yellow and irritation to make absence
better; where land becomes louder
and memory clouds with pollen,

swaying judgements, wresting
        world to water.

Impressions

At intervals in the mat of chest-high weeds
that cover the block are impressions
of rest and hesitation, body-shaped hollows
where roos have considered it safe

enough to rest, arrest movement or set
hiatus carving out green walls and those
secure feelings we hang on to in our own beds,
our own rooms. Examining these,

I am wary of kangaroo ticks but follow
branching lines of the bubble chart
with each offshoot tangent or idea
that grows and grows just as grass

dries and dies off, woven edifice
I cut away to reveal soil skin their feet
will gently embrace, big toes inscribing
knowledge of when it was safe,

as they rested in this or that place
longer than summer can allow, when
seeing too far they will scatter fast.

Building (Extension)

buildings expanded and collapsed alternately
— THOREAU, *Walden*, 'The Bean-field'

The yearly movement around the sun
is exemplified in the building and not
in the permission to build. The boxes

have been ticked but one man's steady
labour has tracked the sun: short days
cold to the bone, long hot days strain

shade to breathe; perspiration
parodies diminishing plenitude
of rainwater tank, the zest

and immediacy of its contents,
not quantity, which is less day
by day. Just outside seismic

intensity, tremors still touch
the hills, the concrete pad: edge
of scarp that has you glancing

out at what has been and could be,
when the sea rises, making an island
of house and contemplation.

The building has contracted
and expanded alternately, bedrooms
added, shelves for books, electrical

connections where there'll
be no electricity. That spark
of language that sparked

a craving for intensity
when intensity is the creature—
possum, roo, shingleback—

moving slowly past the front door
when there is no 'front' or 'back',
just points of the compass.

A greeting, enfilade, vestibule
of activity: *that* door. The din of birds
a disruption to the passage

of warplanes overhead, training
to make a mark, a strike against threats
always being determined.

Beans and Jam Tree Gully

—THOREAU, *Walden*, 'The Bean-field'

The first beds I plant here
will be beans: broad beans. I'll
carry original seed straight
from my old garden. A fresh
intrusion. Another acquaintance
with weeds: rendezvous, assembly.
There's a cleared space ready
for me to engage with. Bean crop
will enrich soil for the following
year. They are vanguard. They
are reliable. Even when I leave
the old garden fallow they
emerge and we take small
unplanned dinners: their expense.
We take what's needed.
They seem inured and immune
to predators, other than
a black fungus that rides
roughshod and eats leaves.
And cutworms that slice
seedlings from beneath.
But thick planting
thwarts attacks, among
companions. Diversity. Origins.
First place of breaking—passive-
aggressive show-stopper—soil
aggregations of birth on birth:
beans, animals, our Pythagorean
selves, and what I think about
when planting and harvesting: time-

line of ingestion full to valley edges,
more connected than *electronica*   —
biographia hoodwinks us
into thinking broad beans
without liturgy, robust
with cognitive reflection,
planted here among trees
and reptiles and birds and insects
which haven't known them: enough sunlight,
enough parables of cause and effect,
grand impacts.

What Compliments to Nature

Heat stress takes the tops off whole trees:
straggling outreach clawing and offering
no shade; but still alive at the base of trunks
where new growth might be a last gasp or final stroke,
the touching up of chiaroscuro that's not quite right,
the slightest dab of the brush might
bring to light the darkest secret of burgeoning,
swatches of lushness against haze swamping
the valley. But then, it might tip beyond
correction, that each attempt though so delicate
makes worse, until the painting is lost,
trees expended to the very tips
of deepest roots by next summer.
I think an underground stream
has dried or altered course,
taproots have worked hard to illustrate
a surface lie and finally given up the ghost: the cool
deep an inverted canopy never bereft of shade.

Joy

Joy! Sheer joy! Old
trees dying and acacias
thinning, mood decaying,
discovering seedlings merged
with emptiness, scoured
ground: self-sown
out of dormant
deep red below
sand let loose to rise
in breach, outgrowing
hungry roos whose pruning
encourages branching, fulminating
verdant on a hot, hot day
because roots have worked
long, been working away
before the show; let growth
emerge on singular terms,
odds stacked as odds
might stack if given a go:
still tough and driven,
selective, perorating
a precise system but saying.
'we are outside politics,
your speeches your self
where it can't be imagined,
vascular elucidation
staying open to some hope
that all will grow back again,
just the same, same seed,
same dead leaves, dry branches,
the same root of joy,
sheer joy'.

Greedy after this gossip

Sound emphasises the valley and you can't see
who says what—speakers might be a distance

away but you know fragments of their business,
their thoughts. We don't need to meet each other

to know each other. Sheep and goats far down low
are suddenly bleating at your front door though

nowhere to be seen. In the heat that splits trees,
releasing the accumulated gossip of years,

growth rings and that fresh outer layer
of vascular tissue like an Edison cylinder,

and what's more, these trees are filled
with wild bees in waxy hollows. Playing

back the recording you catch heat's cracks
and stresses, the full range of sounds

we send out, half forgetful, sometimes regretful
we said too much, then forgetting the mix,

the swift fall-through of the ringneck parrot
looping our vocalisations: just like the yawn

that articulates as opposed to the yawn
that's a sigh as the sun sets. Eureka!

I echo, another dozen self-sown saplings
discovered today—the bush is regenerating

and the kangaroos gathering in mobs
and selectively eating. Eureka, and history:

cinema newsreel from the days of imperial
consolidation, with their tinny, shrieking

sound tracks, animals dispersing and unable
to lip-synch, graziers and their shock-troops

whooping and philosophising at once,
opening out the spaces to be better heard by,

sounds lumped together to call 'nation'.
But here we speak and await the reply. Listen!

Chaser Bins

Harvest has begun in the drier places
and has stretched its tongue down to where
a damp still gleams on the ears of wheat
when first light disperses bisque and yellow.

It makes me ache. Monoculture is harm,
monoculture is counter to all that is sacred,
growing up out of soil's thin lips. But I am caught
in that beauty, caught in the glow of a wheat sea

about to be drained: the header following
the rise and fall, peaks and troughs of crop,
working hard to keep the stubble a consistent
length, and the chaser bin drivers running

neck and neck to take grain from the header,
from the whale's stomach as Jonah watches on, volume
measured by tank or sack, augered into a waiting truck,
transfer on transfer, auger and spout, elevator

and transfer. It makes me ache. The grain
vulnerable to cracking, and my split personality
of viewing and smelling the harvest, choking
and gleaning a past and a presence from harvest

rolling in: chemical grain I'd rather not purchase,
shelved half-life, markets and fetish. Hard work, stripped
ground, money in the bank if the sky stays clear—
from ear to milling, uncomplicated as it never is,
        eternal wish for plain sailing.

Closing the Gate

It's an expedition, setting
off in the heat, best wait
for evening before battening
down the hatches. The roos sidestep
or leap the fence, which is welcome,
but closing the gate stops cars
spinning in as if it's a road
somewhere, a possibility
rather than a dead end.
You slide on the gravel
going up, even more so
heading back down. The driveway
is a letter S in which the edges
have failed, making gashes and culverts
along the walls of the curves;
when it storms, the water screams
down and drops entire letters
from this alphabet, this written
language we tread cautiously,
looking up and down at each
other through the trees, over
the gravel, the granite,
architecture of valley wall
we close off at nightfall
just after the hills light orange
with kinetic energy of too much
movement through day.

Voices Carry across the Valley

Voices carry across the valley
from incline to incline, vibrating
within the warped v. Repetition
and refrain hoodwink you, listening

to elevated chit-chat or incantation
or invocation of the humdrum voice
of oracle blending human and eagle,
like a rasping seagull, like a griffin

with obsessions and peccadillos,
a darkness peccant and threatening.
In the walls of the v, though apposite,
the lull at the nexus, drainage

makes erosion conflate as words
deflate, risen too high before feeding
back onto our neighbours, though we
might call across 'clear as a bell'

and, despite the distance, greet
each other before high notes
become silhouettes on the lips
of the hills, reminding us all

how far away, how silent
the outside world, blue meniscus
of sky that collapses with night,
bearing down on this valley,

carrying sound in similar
    but different ways.

Past Tense

The early morning was replete with gunfire,
the repetition of a twenty-two from the hill
opposite the reserve, a kid no doubt, a kid
who spurs his scramble-bike through paddocks
when fire-bans are commonsense for anyone else:

last night I went out to locate the source
of gunfire and saw galahs in their hundreds
lift and settle in the trees on our block,
kangaroos thrash through the half-light,

away from the gunfire. There was laughter
and gunfire—teenagers caught in their
gender performances. Everything suffers.
The valley is the microcosm you'd expect.

Language generates nothing as whole trees fall

Language generates nothing as whole trees fall
to harsh winds and corrosive temperatures:
and even recognising this, I centre it on all
our observations, as if allowing for cause

or variation, derivations and attitudes:
to notate with sound we didn't hear, imagine
the phrasing of the split and solitude
of collapse, though collating the sign

and analogies of loss, means a tone-deaf
response from the finest composers or interpreters
of their music. But I won't leave you bereft
of satisfaction: not far from here, down where

rail follows the logic of the brook, I 'watch
the passage of morning cars with the same feeling
that I do the rising of the sun . . .', and catch
the transferral of crop to port, step in feeding

the rich and poor of the entire world. Language
plays its role in conveying sustenance, chemical
responses signed out, translated from forage
to food, unlike the dead tissue of all

those fallen trees, my own autolysis—so alive
the sound of damage and sunlight, to me at least,
keeping an ear out for what we strive to hear
but can't, feeding words into death's trysts.

Contrition is not the sole preserve

Contrition is not the sole preserve of religion—
every step taken up or down this hill brings more
than remorse for what has fallen, each lost angle of growth,
what might have been if our steps weren't sown.

Contrition is not the sole preserve of religion—
and survival is not sin though survival brings loss and a reason
for sorrow; then grazed or mined to the bone, more than survival
is extracted—hills lose while we are value added.

Contrition is not the sole preserve of religion—
a reptile's illustration as it moves through red dust on the hill
configures this—evasion and engagement it might seem to us,
asking for forgiveness though it has vanished.

The Immolation of Imagination

It only abstracts as far
as a twenty-knot northerly
ripping into the over-dry
bushland, into the districts
of wild oats, each strand
a chimney for a furnace—
millions interwoven into
the inverse of a fire blanket.
There's a total ban on vehicle
movement and we sit in the house
apprehensive and cautious
hoping conditions don't convert
speculation into immolation.

See, that's it, there's no
room for imagination when
things are so on edge, prospects
so extreme—no metaphors
to be dragged out of a musical
interlude in an air-conditioned
concert hall or the perfectly
sustained and consistent
temperature of a revered
art gallery, repository
of invaluable truths, insights
into what we are beyond
the drowned or the burnt.

So, we hear trailbikes
hack through the reserve
and I burst out the door
and bolt up the hill, wanting

to stop them, stop the fire
they will spark, that will kill
all that's living other than the
riders, who will probably outrun
the flames on their fast and skilfully
piloted bikes: it's not spite
that has me say this, but something
much bleaker, much darker
than the offerings of fire.

But they are gone
before I can locate them.
And I stand still,
expecting the worst.

An eagle carries
something to its eyrie,
and the vacuum-rush
of the wind stays hot
and dry and empty.
I grip my chest
which convulses:
there are so many
ambiguous ways to die.

Survey

It's been too hot during the day to survey
the block—ornate language doesn't do the trick,
it's a physical, material, and pragmatic performance . . .
not 'radical empiricism', but an act of preservation.

The difference here; the difference elsewhere.
I work this over as I note the fast, hot winds
have brought down two great limbs from the eucalypt
by the tank, the green leaves already seared

and probably 'dead before they hit the ground'.
The water-trough I fill for kangaroos and other
wildlife in this desiccated habitat is almost
dry and what moisture remains informs a bloom

of algae. I clean and refill. Red ants bite my feet
and I carefully brush them away. A hawk
looks for a safe perch to settle for the night.
Each substance 'inheres', or is it 'in which

they inhere'? as William James might attribute
to this wood from the fallen tree, questioning its quality
of 'combustibility and fibrous structure'.
I—*we*—manage our days because of those

attributes, those qualities of burn. I survey
the block in the relative cool of evening
while there's still enough light to make things out:
shape them individually and as an entirety,

into a whole that adds up, is as good as might be,
kept from larger harm, grouped in those days
James lectures us about, phenomena of climate
and gumption to resolve as much as possible.

I entrust to the relative cool of night.

Town Hall Meeting: Minutes

So the fire came in walls of flame
that razed bush and paddocks and sheds
and animals and birds and insects
and entire houses. People escaped.
It was the day of the 'catastrophic'
warning, when we left early morning
for safer ground. We couldn't get home—
roads were blocked and fire out of control,
incinerating the district. Embers flew unseen
to ignite surroundings kilometres
from the fronts. Spot fires. Forty-five
degrees and a nor'-westerly
blowing like a hairdryer on full.
A story of ash binding all other stories
to the ledger: inventories, life-histories,
hard work. We managed to get back next day
taking the side-route through Irishtown.

The midday meeting at the town hall.
Those who've lost houses speak out—
distressed, confused, stalwart.
The head of state has his say
(owning property on the outskirts).
A woman asks when the children she's
minding might be reunited with parents,
trapped in a farmhouse in the no-go zone?
Water-bombers chop and whirr overhead,
you can hear them over the crowd,
over the PA. How do you express
sympathy for loss? You lost and you lost . . . 'but we
still have our lives' . . . Sorry. Thanks. Sorry.

The fire is still burning out of control
but 'contained'. Wide lines make right
angles of the wall. Reporters frantic
about the fringes making human interest
because everybody seems to need it. I find
this disturbing but that's just me. Again,
I am convinced of the gratuitous
nature of the figurative: I retrieve a local
meaning of the word 'conceit' here:
what most of those in town would want
from the word: as in 'conceited',
to make poems so close to the bone,
watching the helitacs across the hills
from highpoint of this land I stand upon,
smoke diluting into blue, false blue
that is, nonetheless, a relief to see, to hear.

I went to that meeting because I felt
I had to, uncomfortable being jostled
as the crowd pushed forward to hear
those from the Shire, police inspector,
FESA official, Premier, his silent
but affirming minister, child protection
officer, those who had lost so much . . .
Apparently, towns recover from such
things . . . events, disasters. Pull together.
Time passes. Diversion. Photographs
taken by those whose names don't seem
to matter as much as they once did.
Is this what we become part of: distress
and a silence that follows?

Urban Attitudes in the Bush?

Fire wardens claim those who want to preserve
trees bring urban attitudes to the bush, themselves favouring
scarified hills and valleys, dust bowls feeding
no flames—the rural way, mission to conserve

a real emptiness colonists brought to country
in their claims it was there to be claimed. When
the 'keep out' threat of 'my field' and my field alone
echoes through councils and those government ossuaries,

titles offices, open space joins open space
and you can see it all spread productively from space, *they*
    might say:
accruals on a planet getting hotter day by day,
with lengthening fire seasons that erase

calendars and equinoxes and cities like London
or Hanoi or Baghdad or Nagasaki or Hiroshima or Dresden:
each street planned with urban attitudes,
each flame risen above the scorched multitudes.

Hair

prolific hybrids hav e been produced
—THOREAU, *Walden,* 'Brute Neighbours'

Surveying the reserve again after hearing gunfire
I come across a large thatch of hair—a headful,
quantity and weight-wise—neatly poised on the fire-
break. I look at it closely—chocolate brown, strands
wavy and of an in-between length. I look around the area,
lightly and hastily. Gunfire persists across the valley.
I've got to tell somebody though I am not sure
what I'll actually be telling them. It is so weird.
And, seriously, disembodied. The looming granite
and concerted York gums provide an atmospheric
part *Picnic at Hanging Rock,* part *Wake in Fright.*
The soil of the firebreak as it winds decisively
down the hill is deeply red but infertile. A stale
blood that nurtures only the specific, the familiar.
The thatch of chocolate brown hair doesn't sit
comfortably. I walk home and convince Tracy
that she should take a look. Absorbing the view,
semi-panorama that catches you, she crouches
and examines the hair. From one side, then another.
It seems to me to take longer than it should,
inducing a form of apprehension. 'I think it's
animal hair,' she finally says. I re-examine
and notice matting and congealing beneath.
Goat. Or an exotic 'item' of stock from a hobby
farm. Hoicked there by a fox. Eagle to line its nest.
Just statements made without conviction. *Possibilities.*
We agree that it's not human—or that it's very
unlikely to be human. And if it were, what would it mean?
Hair on a firebreak out in the bush. Gunfire continuing.

Jam Tree Gully Sonnets with Incidental Rhymes

(I)

> an animal health and vigor distinct from the spiritual
> —THOREAU, *Walden,* 'Higher Laws'

I keep meaning to pick up the now-bleached pelvic
bone of a sheep. It's up the hill, cradled among stubble
and Toodyay stone. A remnant of what happened here
before we took over custodial duties. A harp-shaped bone
others might string and play. I *assume* it's pelvic, related
to the hindquarters. I don't know how I know, though
as a child watching sheep being killed and 'dressed', I might
have asked. My memory is highly selective these days.
I don't really know what to do with the bone, other than
to think it over. I guess that's why I keep meaning to pick
it up, to weave chiasmic lines out of its life-death shape?
Living, it wouldn't have been part of a large sheep, maybe
part of a lamb, which makes contemplation more complex.
It seems resistant in heat—harsh, reflective, less porous.

(II)

> Let us spend one day as deliberately as Nature, and not
> be thrown off the track by every nutshell and mosquito's
> wing that falls on the rails.
>
> —THOREAU, *Walden,* 'Where I Lived,
> and What I Lived For'

I am constantly distracted and doubt there are any
straight lines or mathematical certainties for me to latch
onto; having said this, by way of diversion, I note

that at the same time yesterday I watched two blue
butterflies tango around each other in as precise
a way as I am capable of detecting: within
my threshold it looked like pure choreography: in
the same place, close to the ground below the mistletoe
looking contingent but hardy, parasitic in the acacia
outside this window. There is a profound connection
between mistletoe and blue butterflies. What's more,
the acacia, life-host to mistletoe and performative space
of blue butterflies, is laden with seed pods in its own right,
drawing parrots and many other birds to its abundance.

(iii)

I reiterate, those wedge-tailed eagles are as big as Tim
who is six and quite tall for his age. Their occupation
of the large York gums at the top of the block continues,
and we wake to their wheezing, rasping communications,
utterances just beyond silence and incongruous as you might
proffer, though not like beauty and what we might see as brutal
efficiency: those thin notes just after sunrise as eagles take
to a flock of corellas whose squawks seem torment and agony
before carnage, a premonition or pre-destiny, the elect
sounding out their ascension, knowing a better roost is their
allotment; and so, the eagle-pair weigh heavily on branches,
prepare their eyrie; even kangaroos stay clear, joeys not long
out of the pouch, their voices quiet and elusive, gentle percussion
learnt from cicadas moving between heaven and earth.

Sacred Kingfisher and Trough Filled with Water Pumped from Deep Underground

It is the work of art nearest to life itself.
—THOREAU, *Walden,* 'Reading'

With the record heat I filled one of the three
concrete troughs—mainly for kangaroos
but also for birds and anything else that passes
by. This morning I saw a sacred kingfisher
in an overhanging branch, eyeing the water.
The sacred kingfisher saw me and remained.
That's unusual—they are mostly cautious.
I over-invest the 'sacred' in their name—name
giving, name evoking statistics from those
who've probably not even seen the bird. A small
bird with a large beak that could inflict a lot
of damage on whatever it targets. Proportional
and relative. Its colours are flashy and stunning.
What part do I play in filling the trough, once
for sheep and horses? How much choice
to come and go does the sacred kingfisher
have? Would it be here if the trough was empty?
The valley was quiet in the broadest sense.
I did not know how much noise was within
the bird's head. I thought of Thoreau
thinking of Alexander the Great carrying
the *Iliad* in a special casket. Which now
makes me think of a coffin. Water-troughs
look like coffins, like caskets. I expected
the sacred kingfisher to swoop as if the shallow
water held nourishment. It was dead water
from deep in the earth. The sacred kingfisher

stayed in the branch, seeing the trough
for the coffin it was. The bird looked at me
then looked back to the lifeless surface
of the water. Still . . . so still.

Calm

I've managed to get through today
without a major attack of anxiety:
when the eagle flew out of the gully
the shadow of its wings seemed untroubled,
and sounds in the distance were vague
and damage-free. I even discovered
a sapling I thought shrivelled
and killed off by heat, fatigue
in the roots tapped by sandalwood
forgotten as I discovered a pair
of sandalwoods I'd not known were there.
The evening is mild for this time of year
and the light joins imperfections
and different textures alike. I won't sully
the picture with anxieties I keep at bay,
and will resolve night fraction by fraction.

Reading the Poetry of Arto Melleri and Looking at the Extensive World within the Frame of My Window

My child-self rarely looks back at me.
It's like history, I forget intentionally
   then let it all back in with a rush
   with an intensity that provides
extra facts—stuff not in the records,
not even passed down by word of mouth.

It has been too hot to do much outside
today—I could transpose parts of the Peloponnese
   into the picture, should I want to. Or
   reconstruct the Delphic Oracle
   and instruments specific to that place.
Sounds are both close and distant here
always mediated by irregular trees.

If it's all Apocrypha as Melleri in Venice says,
then we can guess he could never have had
   an idea of here: so what? The black-headed monitor
   I saw slip under the silver shed door
   three days ago is its own chapter:
the left-off books might have begun here
if language led him to believe so.

The window is classical. I will draw
and colour it so there's no see-through,
   but it *will* fill. In here, life
   mimics art and can be just as painful,
but also as beautiful without law and order,
without the past, present, or future.

House at Jam Tree Gully Sestina with Variations

As the sun undermines the hills and walls contract
to hold their tension to hold memory of shape to expand
tomorrow as sun surmounts and drives its vicious heat
into cement into the steel skeleton before evening cool
pulls it back from the brink back into shape with a crack
that mirrors morning's wake-up long before the house settles.

Apprehensive of physical distress we'd hope the house settles
over the entire valley, its skin resistant to aggro, a contract
for harmony or something near as damn it, and if that's not cool
enough for those who say 'if you can't stand the heat
get out of the kitchen', or even those who'd expand
their consciousness at the expense of conscience, or crack

their mother's back as they step across the tiles, or crack
a joke about tree-huggers or, on the flipside, *tut tut* as the sun
    settles
for the moon's position; then Hell! *They* hate nightbirds and
    contract
the exterminator to rid walls and roof of rodents, lay heat
on their slippery tails, or hunt down ferals who swan in a cool
sea-breeze come so far inland over the hills. We hear the house
    expand

and hope for the best while expecting the worst, and we expand
our lungs to hold the cleanest air of the day, and we crack
our knuckles as nervous habit, and a daylight darkness settles
room by room as we close blinds and doors to retain the contract
we've made with our personal demons, souls sold to maintain the
    cool
of night, to prevent it leaking through the slightest crack.

And so embroiled or embalmed in the patina of sweat and heat
we think of the Joneses and the electricity they drink, to expand
carbon credits to buy out the sphere, their sacred contract
with the power company, as if we're holier than thou! Who settles
for discomfort never mind the suffering, as history or a crack
in the house of the world—catastrophe—the peculiar cool

of death before bodies heat and bloat in the sun—the cool
of the penumbra where all nameless things wander and graze in
    heat
that's not quite there, the insulation of elegies fails as ghosts
    expand
against design, the most carefully considered architecture will
    crack
and the stress placed on the living and the dead unsettles
lines between them, between us and the house and valley's
    contract.

None of us holds by that contract and knows the evening cool
to be a deception that will expand as much as iron roofs in the
    heat,
and that ants spilling through cracks will go to ground and settle.

Red Shed

who built our red barns so admired as emblems

—HAYDEN CARRUTH, 'Marshall Washer'

People hereabouts distinguish 'our' place
by the massive red shed that pronounces
a ledge hacked into the hillside: erected
by the previous 'owner', it yells cultural
anomaly across the valley: I know how
much she loved horses and dedicated
it as a stable, but I am not sure if she ever
visited America and drew inspiration
from the red barns of folklore and utility.
After years living in red-barn mid-Ohio,
we knew what red barns said to locals
and visitors alike. Here and now, they say:
sticks out like a sore thumb! Or: hey,
you know the place, the one with the dirty
great red shed! The air force use it to sight
for bombing runs. Pure terror. In truth,
it's a placid red, though the horror
of hunkering down in bush, of wanting
not to be noticed, makes it anathema.
Each day it holds sunlight between
itself and an imaginary horizon
that curves with the hills overlooking
the greater Toodyay valley. Imagine
the structure of what would have grown
there if the red shed hadn't staked
a claim? The run-off from its gently
pitched roof, the red music it makes
in high winds, bleeding arteries
that feed reservoirs we drink from.

This memory of America won't depart,
and the red colorbond steel that holds
a postcard portrait, folklore that makes work
and horses and a shelter for all weather
speaks resistance: in the worst fires
it *will* buckle and melt, but the sum
of history, its loud declaration, remain.

Inside the Red Shed

> **But let me tell you how it is inside those barns.**
> —HAYDEN CARRUTH, 'Marshall Washer'

Woodwork masking red metal with high eaves
that could be converted into a loft but cradles electrics,

hay pitched and packed in corners and stalls
wooden and symmetrical and just communal enough

where mares were favoured, the equipment
of horse-keeping a metaphor for being kept by horses.

This is no longer a horse property and the whispers
are of rodents and snakes, and to open the grand doors

of the red shed is to wonder what to make of it, spirits
so imbued no matter how sceptical you are.

Conjure no horses and no horse activities and no
husbandry of horses, washed and rubbed down

fresh from their workouts. Strange how you hear
Beethoven's *Ghost Trio* at work on the senses, its hidden

and never-spoken air of horses, undertones and palpitations
of ghostly hormones. Last year I reviewed a performance

of *Equus*. Last year one of my students did a piece
of creative autobiography on horses *by* horses. She knew

how much she couldn't say. The omegas of horseshoes
are still imprinted in the soft floor of the shed's theatre,

text colourless. What went on in there still goes on,
deny it if you can. I wish this red shed were gone,

hillside restored to its pristine apparitions of *prior,*
native vegetation holding and hiding animals

that cannot be shod, that refuse to tolerate
properties of a shed-stable, its cares and investments.

Jam Tree Gully Awaiting Diagnosis: a run

In pursuing trailbikes through the reserve,
running a gradient steeper than confidence,
heat so much larger than the materials
of my body, my heart struggled and my mind
blurred over and is growing more smothered
and confused by the day. What the doctor
suspects was a 'mini stroke event', or
a vessel burst in the brain or severe
heatstroke, awaits definitive diagnosis.
Now I can't walk further than the watertank
which by the algae on its side seems down
to its last fifth, with a bobtail tucked under
a rock that sits by the tank's curve for no reason,
or the single kangaroo in the tank's shade,
so easily frightened, rising up to full stretch
and hissing—alone now . . . yesterday
there were two, before gunfire in the reserve,
shooters gone before they could be seen
and the corpse of roo gone too, as if
it never were. Now I can only look down
the hill at trees struggling against the longest
run without rain, almost dying off like me,
to be frank, and giving no kudos or emphasis
to the pronoun outside my own self-concern
which is natural enough. Two sandalwood
saplings were eaten down a few days ago,
by the kangaroos when they were plural,
I'd imagine. I don't mind that the saplings
were eaten, and nor should I, but it's a sign
or an omen or a symptom we might apply
to landowners in the valley who see saplings
as prosperity, become extensions of their desire

to profit. For them, the ingestion of sandalwood
saplings in a land stripped of sandalwood
in the heyday of 'settlement', is a capital
offence: after all, Australia opposes the death
sentence for humans, though it's happy
enough when its enemies are killed
by judiciaries outside its own. Et al.

In this damaged state

In this damaged state
where vision is narrower
than a window-frame

where trees dust
the bent horizon
and join to make

a hazel sky, I detect
a bird none but I has seen
before: bird

without parents,
without partner,
who will produce

no offspring. Its song
is elaborate, a tight-packed
sonata that works

its data, its ancient
modernism, into my
reception.

In this damaged state
where vision is narrower
than the window-frame

I see past perceptions:
light that charges
trees and birds

extracts its needs,
its plangent definition
from their blurring

and precision.

A Jam Tree Gully Sheaf

THE WAY OF THORNBILLS

1.

Yellow-rumped thornbills
assemble downhill,
setting off as a group
to cover *territory*:
their stations arc
from gully York gums
up to jam trees on the bank,
then over to dead
or partly dead
York gums on breakaway;
there, preternatural granite
has been broken down
by lichen: shedding scales, flesh
eaten away. Intense
in lower branches, vocalisations
build to operatic, though
higher notes of mezzos
are cut off, shorn away to glitter
in the broad sweep of sun.

2.

Cluster of thornbills—
six or seven with one or more
dropping out on a tangent—
side-trip to reconnoitre
or supplement food stocks,

crossing fence along the reserve,
crams the largest tree
with an intensity impossible
to transcribe. Briskness
is outside behaviour. Meeting
or hiatus or consensus
makes curve around the heaviest
granite boulders:
back on 'our' block
where the habit of perching
on wire horizons close and within range
of even the short-sighted
has lessened.
What property *theft,*
what theft *property?*
Interpolate.

3.

Yellow-rumped thornbills
are back where they started:
circuit complete. They disperse
and reunite to repeat the process
three more times that day, today.

4.

Often accompanying thornbills
are the smallest of birds,
weebills. They dip in and out
of the thornbills' route. Subbed.
Groupies. Cross-talkers.
Set shifters.

At night, they find foliage
that cloisters their balled bodies
best, puffing up, preening
small yawps pinpricking dusk.
An ear out for thornbills
and their dawn start.

THE WIDER DISTRICT

Ringneck parrots loop
from hilltop down to gully,
a swinging descent;
emerald-yellow glimmer
collating topography.

MISTLETOE BIRD

Its red chest partakes
in the duress of shadow
amidst mistletoe's
refusal to be labelled
parasite. Those fruits *it* hosts!

ORB WEAVER SPIDER

Her body massive
as Saturn; the male
a small moon. Shiny
as gas giants might
be—to touch her skin
her articulate web,

repulsion and attraction
woven high-tensile;
that trail of waste—
detritus of history
where flight paths
and maps have failed.

BEARDED DRAGON

An isolated
rock—a lone bearded dragon
still as a branch which
we know will sway when the breeze
picks up and the sun is swallowed.

ARRANGEMENT

The crack in the curve
of the great rainwater tank
brews algae and crusts
of calcium that foothold
brown-headed honeyeaters

tonguing cool water
up where water shouldn't be;
not taxidermy,
nor the dry arrangement
they're set against: branch, leaves,

an entire stunted
tree under a dusty glass
dome: an arrangement
for future generations
to wonder at.

NEST

Bullants are cautious
in their strength—those wide entries
and exits are safe
as churches but also as
vulnerable; their nests gape

close to a tree trunk
and we might read into them
the world that is mouth
and machinery of tongue
and teeth and the speech of bite.

MAGPIE CLAIMANTS

The psychology
of boundary, zone, region
and territory;
to harry the intruder,
keep threats to a minimum

but to recognise
the same steps being taken
across their country;
don't doubt rivalry of songs
where title subsets their space.

A SOLD sign has gone up on the eleven acres across the road, and I've been dreading it. Who will come with what poisons? What run-off?

I check the hydrography—culverts and drains along the roadside: they'll cope unless there's a deluge: then it will sheet down across asphalt, across firebreaks, washing the hill. If we'd had money we'd have bought it just to prevent this happening, this damage we know will come. But to own too much land is wrong. To own land at all is wrong. You can't own land. It's not even a question of property and theft because there can only be custody.

Up the hill, a giant wedge-tailed eagle. So close. It opens its beak and gapes. When it hops from one thigh-thick branch to another, the entire tree sways. It is that big and decisive. He and I know something about the vulnerability of this place. We're both big blokes but that means nothing. Just as fragile, just as ready to fall. Neither of us is giving in, despite this knowledge. There's nothing anthropomorphic about this and if you can't tell why then we've reasons to fear what you've in mind for here or wherever you read this declaration of independences.

Eternally Green

Eternally green patch of ground
In cleft of dead hills where a windmill
Draws water against an arid tract
Deep from a subterranean channel;

Overflowing it nourishes a quagmire,
Rhizoid triangle with sublittoral hint, creep
Of lushness against the arenaceous tableau
That shows it up while two thin sheep

Graze constantly and never sleep,
For night brings black-green feed
Compelling them to chew to keep
Up with growth that won't go to seed

And shines intensely green even when sun
And wind ignite surroundings, the price
That's paid for an anomalous eternity
Where two sheep stay thin in paradise.

'Any prospect of awakening'

for Tracy

I receive the news like an imprint,
an autoimmune system I lay over my own,
counting out nodal points. Fresh
roo tracks up by the gate, direction
of breakaway textures description:
to instil enthusiasm cuts both ways
in sheer physical exertion of noting
shadows through valley, exuberance
of dryness thinning the living, transcribing
its tragedy on this fixed model we've
agreed upon: feed this unnatural fixation
on place down to chips of rock, dried
filaments of moss to be loved, inducing
illness or 'Stendhal Syndrome', where art
works out of what's below, dead passages
from where roots have tried too hard
to reach any prospect of awakening
that's held onto, and you'll tell me it's so . . .
what I guess to be out there, what we know.

I had wondered about the signs of burning

I had wondered about the signs of burning—
sandalwoods whose sap exudings had crumbled to dust,
charred trunks at seemingly random points
while others fresh with unsinged bark, and some deep
burnings where rings of a tree had been turned
inside out, excoriated, left ill-fitting within the chimney
of a long established tree. There are other small signs
as well—how ants admonish a track, or where moss
might or might not persist past the driest edge
of summer. None of it made sense. The house shows
no signs—the old core of the house as it is now—
of fire, of giving up the ghost. But there's a matte
to the sheen of paint to suggest fire or the sun
came close. We know there are lightning strikes:
I have seen the result. But then we hear that some
years ago a 'new neighbour' over the hill mowed violently
on a hot brittle day, kindling wild oats and spilling fire
up over and down the valley. It ran fast, apparently,
and the lines of rock the knuckles of granite pushed
it away in places, as did the vacua of vegetation
enacted by dominant red ants. And firebreaks.
The fire shaped with the hills' shape but stayed low
to the ground. Almost prescribed, but not quite,
as anomalies and paradoxes and tautologies
increased and bent older neighbours' memories,
shared and reformed by newer neighbours.
Regardless, we bring a knowledge of such catastrophes
from our old place, and they serve us well
and serve as warnings here, too, and we know
fire is just around the corner, the house's shadow.

'For the root is faith'

—THOREAU, *Walden,* 'Economy'

There is always dust in the air
and that gives us this peculiar
but lustrous blue: a warped faith
filters it out so it feeds
as if your lungs are drawing purest
air possible. All is fed by roots
that if not dormant wait for adequate rain
to break surface, to sink in,
to wallow about rigorous membranes.

For the root is faith, here, outside,
and inside me: it's not malignant
though just as well could be,
but its lexicon and concordance
with a taste for perfect structure
of oxygen, and what it grabs onto
drags deep down where you'd suffocate
if covered over, or left to the reflex
to draw in and fill yourself with black light.

On Large Farms Nearby

our only field known to fame ...
—THOREAU, *Walden,* 'Where I Lived, and What I Lived For'

The fields here muzzle around copses
of wandoo or York gums and look calm
as green undercurrents slowly and gently
sweep beneath the aurulent stubs of dead crops,
but foreboding rather than comfort comes up
out of this chartreuse sweep which would mollify
our casual glances, or settling within the cycles
of production; this bareness in its hints and glints
is more than allusion to distant arcadias,
much more in its fresh or spent flags for lives
lost: all who moved or stood still, affixed, all
who thought or dreamed or kept their manner
silent to my—our—way of hearing. It is so still
today the air cloys about our eyes and we squint
because of glare. We look hard at what might
have been. We listen and taste the air. Our skins
tingle with a sense of being able to move away
and forget before we've imagined or remembered,
sheep quaint in their march to the troughs,
windmills drawing water from an aquifer
near spent though it recently rained.

Rock Overturned by God-Knows-What

Up the sloping paddock, you triangulate
a corner post. You've learnt this from
watching sheep. And common sense. And just
a bit from studying physics. And the feel
of slippage under your feet. And way up
you hesitate, as if something isn't right,
which it isn't. You stare at it in the face.
A rock overturned by God-knows-what.

It's too heavy to be tripped over unnoticed,
and even in the dry, shows haunted stalks
of grasses that appear dead on top, in fact
stalks that have become roots, translucent
underlife that draws blood from stone,
makes water fill the mouth while sucking rock.
So fresher than night in this glare the result,
a rock overturned by God-knows-what.

Pricked Fingers

My fingers prick and ache as I type—
I've been pulling caltrop out of the gravelled
sideslope of the road that curves
past the front of the 'property'
and its long drawn-out irony.

Through cotton gloves the underworld
spikes of caltrop fruits—thorns that puncture
further into the bloody layers below your
surface. It takes the hand where
designed for the foot—'foot-trap'—

anti-personnel elephant downer—
my own grabbing and tearing at the rosette
winding dead-sun like out of taproot.
Moving faster or slower through differing
layers of resistance, that prostrate

leap, that levitation towards
your glorious beseeching—shit!
making confession or therapy
out of task, wishing to spike
memory or tap the forbidden:

but there's not much more in there,
in me, to bleed out of such narrow
if painful points of entry, departure.
You want revelation in the face
of pain, as if bitumen or individual

balls of gravel might reflect back more
than the sum of what you are. It's a dangerous
time in your labours of love, your duty
to stop the spread. Though what's altruism?
And what's recovered, anyway? A car

pulls over, beside you, in the middle
of nowhere. What's the matter, mate? Just
pulling caltrop from the roadside. Good
on you, mate, knowing the risk you take
to mind and body, those fingers

wrecked by pinpricks less likely
to touch lightly those deepest arteries
and veins, those sensitive spots
we labour to cover, we push down
into the previous night's dreams.

Kangaroos in torchlight

Stillness makes you shiver inside, skin
unmoving; there is no part of our biographies
feeding the torchlight, only the kangaroos
trying to look gently past the flickering beam
at what's moving, what makes light out

of darkness; they don't get to select
their deaths and call it 'madness' or 'okay,
I took the risk', they just try
to stay out of its reach. In this
is the only immense spirituality

I believe, walking the long road
up the hill to close the gate, to close
in and protect what I'd like to think *they*
pass over, like our oversubscription
to the soul's persistence, or that some

memory will stick to rocks and soil,
stay close and bear light that seals
a nightworld in place, that we might absolve
the shaky clinginess of gravity: rather, all
imagined is partial indifference

of kangaroos by torchlight, stilled
to graze the dead grass of Elysian Fields
where nothing can die again, and few
will head back to that overwhelming light
that weighs so heavily on the living.

'whose discordant screams were heard long before'

—THOREAU, *Walden,* 'Winter Animals'

after the annual district 'fox-cull competition'

Red fox on red firebreak emerges after the slaughter,
After the killings corellas hesitate in their flocking instinct,
Whose discordant screams were heard long before.

I make my outline against early morning, take a splinter
Of each shadow to ensure that all our fates are linked,
Red fox on red firebreak emerges after the slaughter.

Whether or not I believe, I agree that it strives to rain at Easter,
And apportion prayers to sky and ground and even blood—each
    distinct—
Whose discordant screams were heard long before.

It is said the fox that screams is never noisier
And that a flock of corellas is rarely silent,
Red fox on red firebreak emerges after the slaughter.

I have stories to go by, knowledge by which to enter,
But fear that outcomes are almost impossible to predict,
Whose discordant screams were heard long before.

Which is why through haze I see white as red, as colour,
And allow myself to be distracted by sunlight on a sun skink,
Red fox on red firebreak emerges after the slaughter,
Whose discordant screams were heard long before.

Night Explosions

The house shudders and pings on its concrete pad
perched on the hill-ledge, the red shed on the terrace
above, reverberating to set up a sick harmonic.
Shaken, we check on our seven-year-old but he's still
asleep. I run out into the night that seems darker
than it is: cloud riding roughshod over half-moon,
almost a strobe but powered by solar panels: reflection.

On the hillside in the uncertain dark another explosion,
so massive I slip on the gravel and my tinnitus comes on,
a song I can't get rid of. From the north-west. I return
to the house as steadily as I am able, bracing against
nothing, at intervals, in case another barrage erupts.
Tracy calls through the window: the ranger says
it's the army over thirty ks away. Playing war games.

It's ANZAC Day this weekend and they're celebrating
the vast casualties of past wars, ahead of schedule.
Let's not pretend it's anything more than a shindig
for guts and glory, the arch adrenaline of remembrance
projected forward, the young kept on the boil. Standing
here as these explosions go off, contorting the valley,
you'd know that shell-shock is the best-case scenario.

My Auntie Dulcie in the Retired Servicemen's Home
is starting to forget things, but not how she loathes war.
She is the oldest living widow of a First World War
Gallipoli Campaign veteran. She is considered 'red'
by the aged soldiers and wives of soldiers she shares
the bunker with. But she has friends there and is popular.
So many different kinds of nightmare to compare.

Night explosions unsettle the shape of the land. It is fit
to burst. Kangaroo tracks criss-crossing block and reserve
bind them together. But there's a perverse stillness
as the ground shudders, tingling nerve damage after
an accident. And surreally a pair of ducks fly past fast
towards the distant coast, low and hard to where
the sea pounds the shore, waves loom crest on crest.

'Heaven is under our feet as well as over our heads'

—THOREAU, *Walden,* 'The Pond in Winter'

With an axe and a bucket and a thirst
that will smash the mirror, crack reflections
quicker than look at them. Beneath, the water;
though here it's hundreds of feet down through rock
nigh hard as drillbit. The world's diamonds are running out
and what's left drills into freshness, the heaven
beneath our feet that will run out. Winter approaches
as winter does and there's still no rain of substance,
nothing that sustains washing and drinking, keeps
trees alive. No crops will be sown for some time
to come. Irony of fogs and freeze-dried dust
is not the irony of thirsting in a mélange of ice
and snow and water under the thick mirror
and marmots with eyes closed: here, as here is,
the roos come close to the house sensing water,
the ground bare and even dew vanishing before
satisfying their need. Dew, that nineteenth-century
faux pas, that saturation of its time, convention
to position a tone, a mood, a diamond sparkle
is all you're going to get, extracting water
as you can, living the dream, drinking an image.

'I left the woods for as good a reason as
I went there.'

—THOREAU, *Walden*, 'Conclusion'

In the saga of living, Tim labels the thinned bush
on the block as 'the dark woods': he doesn't fear it,
but rather relishes intrusions and expeditions, and the deeper
it gets as closer to the floor of the valley we descend,
the *better* it is. He likes fear and wants to sound like
Vincent Price. If he can't make it as an actor or writer
he will do voice-overs, he says. But when he plays
out on the 'estate' by himself, he knows the boundaries
set make sense, though he tests the edges like habit.
Enlichened rocks, twisted trees, steel posts left over
from internal fences pulled down. I watch him
at a distance, marking a boulder as centre, his excursions
fan out, echo into the clearing and perimeters, his eyes half-
turned to the dark woods beyond. He needs them
to enrich the open spaces, to know fear is at hand,
but to see everything approach from a long way
off: time to react, time to take diversive action.
And as red-capped robins rustle about him, more
untroubled than they usually are by the presence of humans,
he takes them into his confidence and they dart
into the dark woods with his messages, his efforts
to make contact, and come out bristling with tales
he understands and translates, sagas he might be part of.

Mea Culpa: Cleaning the Gutters

Not quite believing that rain would come
in thimblefuls never mind buckets, pre-
dawn deluge, cracking of the skies
with essence of light made out of absolute
darkness, took me unawares. I'd learnt
not to believe in forecasts, to doubt
even the particular movements of birds.

Not quite believing that rain would come
I'd left cleaning the gutters, while lamenting
the emptying of the Great Tank down to its final
rung, or reaching its echo full-blown, grown
to fill an emptiness, replete with sound,
those final drops of silt and leaves that settle
having found their way through pipes to brew.

Not quite believing that rain would come
I had to wait until the last gasp of thunder,
brace the ladder, and work my way around the house,
circumnavigate and excavate the gutters: black silage
scooped and flopped to the ground—inky and indelible
even on sand. And then down to the trap to release
the filth, and scouring even the Great Tank's top itself.

Not quite believing that the rain would come
I lose time and water and watch taps flow brown.
Mea culpa, Thomas the Doubter, and whatever negative
affirmations run through my head. Cut by the tin roof,
I have only one hand free to revise what's been
hastily done: bloody hand dangling at my side,
useless and polluting as I waver near rain and sky.

On Being Asked to Join the Coondle-Nunile Volunteer Bush Fire Brigade

> be lofty enough to create some obscurity overhead,
> where flickering shadows may play at evening
> about the rafters
>
> —THOREAU, *Walden,* 'House-Warming'

In painting many views of the same scene
fire short-circuits desire—its shifting intensity
and reliance on fuel and the inconsistencies
of that fuel, weather conditions and designs
to control to thwart its inclinations indicate
that painting is more than time of day or mood
or even change but rather of the moment as the moment
is tested in its materiality in its very existence. And so
the volunteer fire brigade coming in under a Shire order
and burning the eleven acres opposite us, sending
the hilltop into crown-death, its tension its extreme
possibility of fire iceberging the valley with our
place first off the rank, just below the fire waiting
to happen, lit to be incendiary in personality
profile: how do I illustrate flames against the sheen
of the red shed, an angled reflection that cancels
out its mirror face with blowsy heat that has you
turning away, blushing at shadows in the rafters,
hooded with fastsmoke so obscure under cloak of sky.

So one of the firemen comes down to me standing
concerned against the fence. I say, I hope it doesn't jump
the road and he points to the fire trucks and their sarcastic
loads of water, and adds that his own house isn't far
enough away to escape such anger. Why not join
the brigade? he asks, as the fire he helped ignite

runs rapidly away. I want to answer that painting fire
is a tenuous art, that we necessarily recover all fires
we've seen—those contained in fireplaces, seen loose
in paddocks and forests, making chimneys out of ancient
trees, headlines and news features. Simultaneity,
I answer, and he looks at me as if I might be mad,
even dangerous. Fire is to be feared, I say. It is never
under control. Fire can never be painted, it's only
a memory of what *was* flashed over the paper,
at the moment of feeding. It eats too much, and re-
growth is a choice it allows, not one we empower;
burning where you will to stop burning emptiness,
flickering shadows singing the sky in forgery

CODA

Harrowed hilltop in black before ash
smelling burnt grass and burnt water
when water has vanished for drinking.
Birds flee *here*. Fulminate. Flies from lashings

of wildoats wicked: glossary, concentration
of elemental habitation, de-green rhetoric
of smell, taste, because we stay here, move
close to be singed, and copy-edit back.

A Set of Images Makes the Day

1. Gradient washes fast as ice
the deterrence of iceberg rocks,
granite knuckles, gnomologic.

2. In ground tough as flint
objection sparks steel of shovel;
and yet, damp bloody soil.

3. Bottlebrush against fencepost
to deliver bird and insect fodder.
Array of habitat. Catafalque to fairground.

4. Star pickets are half stars if our
emblems on school paper are real
representations of who we are:

5. Dozens of star pickets slotting
into each other, plethora of steel.
Eyelets and dropforge out of dark.

6. Shaky with work, the parrots' tonguey
chirrup becomes a piping: I am their
movie: they shimmer more when still.

Whang!

—THOREAU, *Walden,* 'Winter Animals'

A dry winter but there's still enough green
on the ground, enough to push the cycle around.

Each day the report of a gun. Different guns
cross-talking. Striking up a conversation.

The pen might be mightier than the sword,
but the gun is signature and signatory.

The pattern of rifling takes precedent
in a world of patterning. It signs off

in the reserve, and again. A debate, arguing.
Whang! the beast rolls over dead on the ground.

Whang! the beast rolls over and hobbles away.
There's enough bush to get lost in here—the injured

come our way. Winter sun soothes emotional scars,
reflects in the hunter's glasses. *Whang! Whang!*

It's musical and masturbatory. A winter fecundity.
On the lookout for victims, I walk the hills quietly.

Away from the sun, the mossy floor resurges.
The ground I walk heavily pushes back softly.

Bonewrest (Jam Tree Gully)

Where *here* was Sleepy Hollow
and skulls adorned the gate:
horned starers whose prophecies
were lodged in edgy eye sockets:
the owner tossed neatly sawed
bones to her dogs. Today, I set
out to collect offcuts in a sack,
send them to a different rest.
What the segments belonged to
was large, dominant. Thick
as my wrist, finely honeycombed
on the cut surface. Strewn in dry soil,
in the wetter soil clasped
by green weed and breathing
down hard, having truck
with nematodes. Living bones
belated or reincarnated
as themselves, but living still,
sculptures in their randomness,
though no dog drops one
without recall, without purpose.
What stories I step into
or out of are mediated
by these bones. But I try
not to read into their scattering
more than needs be, more
than they offer.

Stubble Quail at Jam Tree Gully

Cats and foxes roam the block: we
see them occasionally, and their scats
and footprints constantly. At night
they speak against each other, competing

for what's to be got. Rodents here
keep a low profile and we don't see
many. And with the drought, more
and more shelter for birds and animals

is dying off. Even mid-winter green
on the ground is low. So, today,
with the sun close to the brow of hill,
and my being down in Bird Gully

I was shocked at seeing a family
of stubble quail. They eyed me, then
vanished into a hollow between fallen
trees, a cocoon for a nest just beyond

a fox's muzzle, a cat's paw.
This is not quails' usual nesting
method, and clearly some kind
of adaptation to circumstances

of threat and impoverishment
has taken place. Whether it's
Lamarckian or Darwinian shouldn't be
debated. If it catches on throughout

the wheatbelt then come and speak
to me about origins, how characteristics
are acquired or begotten. Noting their
wary expressions, I chose to leave.

Skins

in silence while he skinned the fox
—THOREAU, *Walden,* 'Winter Animals'

Upping the ante is participation.
Just the looking into old ways in museums.

A single Kelpie rounds a mob of sheep
from deep inside the paddock. It yaps.

The clover harvester has round hooves
of sheep skin that collect the burrs

with a nagging whirr. Fox skins
are treated in sheds and I remember

eyes filled with slivers of light.
Some hunters spread skins on walls

others dished them out for shoulder
fashion, rough 'n' ready. 'Hides',

when collected for bounty. *Romantically,*
'pelts'. And the fat, tepid between skin

and flesh, whatever the beast, drying
stiff as boards. And the polish of cowhides,

you could see your reflection, or
curl up in embryonic comfort, to be

reborn in your wilderness, bliss,
or city cultural richness; a drink,

a show, a dinner to digest,
snug deep within your skin.

Battening Down

The first big front of winter
has crossed the coast. It will rise
up over the scarp and lose a little
strength but when it hits us in the north
-eastern corner of the hills, chevroned
in this valley, it will have enough strength
to tear off roofs, annihilate trees. Two
or three hours' grace, if we're lucky.
The skies are still cold and blue,
but a light wind works the tassels
of dead leaves hanging from drought-
ravaged eucalypts. Everything
is so brittle it will crumble before
being made subtle by heavy rains;
expected. Such waitings are loaded
with too much of the impending
and fleeting at once, the confusion
of waking then returning to sleep,
mere fact of earth falling to the sun
without heat, rushing outwards
from the Big Bang; together. Anxiety
is why I befriended cosmologists;
ambiguity is why they befriended
me. I must go out onto the block now
to secure loose objects, and when
I descend over the false horizon
of hillside, I will think back over
what I have passed and how it will
look, after the storm. I expect to have
made shelter before the front hits,
everything battened down, but
a variety of outcomes is possible.

'Now only a dent in the earth marks the site of these dwellings'

—THOREAU, *Walden,* 'Former Inhabitants;
and Winter Visitors'

Trench. Excavate. Layer. *Paleo-*
up to a point. Loot provenance.
Overburden trek over, hesitate.
Unearth. Disinter. Absentee
stake-holders tenement arbitration.
Squat import to standardise.
Clean and display. Outbuilding
dents while great house stands:
murders and accidents, grand
occasions accounted for annual
takes and land offer reward
hedge botanise granted imported
iron sheets (galvanised) rusted
away. Here, Royd Nook. Un-
Yorkshire, late labour. Ticket-
of-Leave. Segues into other
narratives too. 'Coolies', 'navvies',
states comprehensive overview
in partial collusiveness. Sign says,
'Site of'. Sign fireplace last stand,
out of the Convict Hiring Depot,
shade and savage sun.

Disturbing the Ashes

As I drew a still fresher soil about the rows with my
hoe, I disturbed the ashes of unchronicled nations
—THOREAU, *Walden,* 'The Bean-field'

Broad beans are coming through strong
despite rain-lack and despite roos
taking heads off so they double-sprout:
fine, it should work like this. Roos shit
and fertilise: what falls and spreads 'naturally',
unhindered in its progress, is fine by me.
Rain is supposed to be on its way
so I am taking a risk and preparing
a potato patch next to the beans: hell
knows why, as the soil is fired clay
and stones, the tubers will have nowhere
to grow, and where they do will entail
alternative sculptings or deformities
depending on your point of view. But the
real focus of this conversation with you
is to note (like an anniversary) that in digging
I broke through a layer of ash and charcoal,
shattered a neatly defined layer of incident
or action. Knowing what we know of the fire
that rushed through the area those years ago
it's a fair enough assumption that this layer
embodies 'what stood here before', but a layer
that redresses wood and soil and stone
to claim another way of making history
where history is an imposition. How does
Thoreau go on, hebephrenic when the world
closes in and the body fails? He says, 'bore
the marks of having been burned', enculturing

and recycling the cause of his presence: most
natural thing in the world, paint from the new
hoe altering the chemical balance where
ash is disturbed and particles embroil.

Gala Days

On gala days the town fires its great guns, which echo like popguns to these woods, and some waifs of martial music occasionally penetrate thus far.

—THOREAU, *Walden*, 'The Bean-field'

The valley walls can't hold water
but sound reverberates and carries
far down; on gala days the town
twelve kilometres away unleashes
fireworks and speeches, reanimates
troopers and convicts, makes allusion
(but only just) to warriors who resisted,
and only because it fits a martial
theme. The big guns at Bindoon
are booming again, celebrating training
and tactics and battles desired. We
shake to our foundations and the valley
throws it around. On gala days
it's not unusual to see the army deploy
vehicles and soldiers, perky or solemn
depending on the celebration. This weekend
gone, a big day on the calendar: the Avon
Descent, white-water race down through
the hills to the city, but this year
there's almost no water in the river.
Still, the gala rolled on, toasting
sand and rocks, clamouring over
dry riparian quasi-reality. We heard
the revellers, distantly, but stayed
away, glancing to the skies for rain.
Neither praying nor unpraying.

Disturbed Ground

Heaped earth, hillock from hill
hollowed, dull lump among peaks
of valley, gravel and clay, laterite
toss-pot embroidered with concrete.

But from within spring robust
saplings of acacia, markers not nipped
off at base by marsupials. Wind-
vanes and defiers of dry winters:

redolent sheen of soft knife-leaves,
harbinger understones as every mound
has its congealing heart: grain
pearled in rolling and scraping,

formula of asides in generating
disturbed ground. Space for the dead
is shrinking as the living close in:
fertile places lifeless, blank.

Four Scenes

1.

I walk down the drive
just before evening: leaving
out the birds and insects I see,
the hint of larger animals,
I have colours and shapes
at angles, blurred,
confrontational; the smell
is of over-ripening grasses
and their drying, and that's
also the sound.

2.

Golden whistlers, honey-eaters, red-capped robins,
weebills, yellow-rumped thornbills, fly-catchers,
all pushing their songs to the limit: clouds
and bandwidths, no static. And the machinery
I introduce into the mix counters nothing,
hearing above my earplugs, feedback
inside my head, I don't note
this as fact, but somebody tells me
what I can't know, senses shaken.
A mouse shot out from near my feet:
I didn't hear it but saw it through my visor:
even the smudges of sap flung up
from cut grass couldn't deceive me.
All I can tell you is my gratitude
deeper than mantra, that the mouse

survived the horror of the steel cutter,
its deadly high pitch snarl, driven
by a shrill but muscular motor.

3.

We've been through two seasonal cycles here
but the seasons don't add up; I can't co-opt
the Nyungar six seasons either. Dry is the word
it all pivots on, if I want to convey what it's like.
You don't need to be more precise than this last phrase.
What it's like is a tired body, the weariness
that is perverse comfort because it eliminates
thinking, even hunger. To a point. It enacts
'payment', though the cloudless skies
fill you with something at night: massive
and bright even when the moon has waned
to nothing, and the valley would interrupt
perfect vision—the all-encompassing view.

4.

Most of the soil was scraped
from the firebreaks last year.
It's a thin-skinned hill.
The shire wants nothing but dirt
or rock for three metres in,
right round the large rectangle.
Trees are anathema. George,
a local truckie with a front-end
loader, says he can scrape where
there's nothing left to scrape.

Fire makes its own ecologies
and mind-sets. Sceptics or not,
he'll do it if we change our minds:
a bottle of Jacks and he's anybody's.

Pressure at the Boundaries (of Jam Tree Gully)

> and the second year was similar
> —THOREAU, *Walden,* 'Spring'

As when heat brings buckles and folds to asphalt,
So the boundaries of the block are with pressure
Of compliance; the grass-crown of hill beyond is orange
With poison, glib statement of absentee land-
Lords; to the east, the live-in neighbours
Graze sheep on firebreaks hours after spraying.
The stereotypes are shooting up the valley. *Phwyt. Phwyt.*
The wildcat is hiding or sheltering inside the granite. *Spit. Spit.*
The pressure has remodelled my plastic emotions.
I avoid some places because the death of trees
Is overwhelming—groundwater vanquished
And surface evaporated. I have to adopt
Or reconcile an accommodating *spirituality*. But
The blossoming trees that remain have dozens
Of bird species rerouting grief: birds dragged
Into relief, agenda of pressure. Brighten
Cautiously? Parody *and* indulge the vision,
Like Pushkin with *Ruslin and Lyudmila*: science
And magic, chivalry and the military (army and air force
On the far side of the forest). And love. I don't
Dwell at the centre, or slightly off-centre
(As the house sits), but gravitate (quasi-scientific
Wish-fulfilment) towards the altering boundaries:
Creation's fictions and aberrant emotions, load-
Bearing fences where trillers and chatterers
Evoke inheritance over history: traits we identify
As marking our survey, spate of hormones
Configuring outlines of Paradise, calm as rout.

Convergence

The grader is cauterising the firebreak
with a cold blade that blazes against the skin;
fire here is more than fear, and bush
invokes a 'preventative' for many. Like tranches
of roadside vegetation cleared—a hundred metres in—
because a roo might leap in front of the car
and damage in dying. Algorithms aren't appeasement.
Grader: sidewalker that walks straight, off-beat
off-centre off the straight and narrow but cutting
clean lines, and A to B debunker, engineered
via crab and boar, snouter of the Levellers,
always in thrall to dozers and uprooters:
I have been edgy all afternoon as it works
the reserve and gravel tracks within The Loop,
scuttling and yet determined up valley walls,
spreading cant and flat-earth manifestoes
to the sides of tracks, creating earthy kerbs;
betwixt two axles the blade remonstrates,
no fuel left for fire to feed off, though pristine
obliterated surface might ice-rink flame's skating
tilt, its roll across to meet the goal opposite;
all development coerces weight and balance
and steadies through counterweight: the grader
is no exception, its destination hard-headed but never
over-balancing. I wonder if my edginess is fear?
A degradation? I shudder. The grader cauterising
the firebreak with cold blade that heats my skin.

Kangaroo Doe

Stepping faster down the hill
I brake against my growing weight
as a doe lifts her head until
our eyes lock and lift full height.

Against momentum I step back
as she drops down to scan
dry ground and sample the lack
of feed within the shadow of a lean

York gum, noon heat bending
round to disturb the cool.
As I step backwards up the hill,
ascend or undo descent, parting.

The Qualities of Sadness

A weird thing just happened:
I felt inexplicably sad when George,
a neighbour I've met once though constantly
heard working, set off in his Mack truck with two
grain trailers. Our meeting was odd—charged with talk
of his drinking and my having long given it up,
a global positioning of local conversation, who
had been in the valley and how long. Rhetoric
flourished and became poetic but he wouldn't
call it that. Tattooed and thick-muscled,
he talked of the harvest to come, how in two
months he'd make a hundred grand to see
him through the thinner parts of the year.
For three days I've heard his compressor
on the wind and have known he's been blasting
his trailers to clean them of gravel and dirt
they've been carting through winter. Instinct
and my dad's life among trucks, a couple
of seasons on the wheatbins and saturation
in The Farm, told me as much. He'd even
sounded me out as we met, he in his ute,
talking out at me preparing to cut the grass.
'You drive a semi?' he asked. A few times
for short distances when I was young. I've
driven box trucks and farm trucks and tractors
though never on the macadam, and never with a licence.
I can handle a Roadranger gearbox: not difficult.
I don't have a licence, I repeat as mantra.
He let it go, no longer figuring me a potential
co-driver, prospective employee. What else
is there to do out in the bush? So just now,
hearing the massive Maxidyne engine idling,

I walked to the top of the block to see him off.
The silver bulldog on the hood glimmered
and alcoholic George, sober as a judge, blasted
the horn to say farewell. An immense sadness
flooded over me and 'the local' meant something
outside geography, outside words. Whoever
he is, I *understand*. Little common ground other
than the valley-side we share, and something
more subtle than degrees of separation.

Entrée

The burrow-building wolf spiders
have colonised ground around the western granites:
a snapped twig by a full-moon entry, open like a one-way
mirror, brings a wolf fast, fangs snapping at the offender;
the glaze of humidity makes drought-sundered life fanatical:
all birds, all insects, marsupials we suspect are extinct,
all flurry and resolve; when we are visited by the man
who writes novels about werewolves I will show him
the wolf burrows. You have to tread betwixt them,
there are so many at this time of year, now.
That's why I don't need to write about more than here.
They are aware of grasshoppers flying and looking like small birds
landing near the entries of their burrows. The lunacy.
In quasi-darkness eight eyes converse solipsistically.
The glare outside is deadlier than you'd think.
To humans, wolf spiders are mildly toxic.

The Roo Killers

They come at twilight every month or so.
They scout the loop in their slow vehicles.
They spy out kangaroos grazing paddocks, the reserve,
They open doors of vans or align pick-ups—dogs
leap and take fences, running down roos
caught by surprise. Sometimes shots are fired
though houses huddle close by. The light dies
as teenagers rush after prey, shrieking with joy,
pumped up like a crossbow bolt, an air gun. If one
of their number regrets later, he doesn't display
his doubts during or after the act. They drag
and hoist the carcass and take it away. I heard
them last night across the valley—earlier
in the day I'd seen a boomer, a doe, and joey
just out of the pouch, sheltering beneath jam
trees—yes, mungart—from the deathsun.
I have not seen them since. Since that last
twilight and its fright. Hurled into the van,
door slammed shut before the distraught
had time to react—anyone who cared
in the valley. Clichés turned a blind eye
as stereotypes played out their complexities,
eh. Rounding the loop, the van sailed past,
tongues hanging from boys too young to drive,
their older patron saint of killing at the wheel,
all scanning what's left of the bush, meat
on their minds, or sport. Dogs barking
from within the metal box where the corpse
might twitch and leak, so near yet so far,
the smell driving them crazy, throttled
by the collars they strain against, to bite

the hand that feeds them a dangerous
option, held back, held back, perverse
inverse of this agony of occupation,
war of attrition we don't fight.

Insomnia at Jam Tree Gully

> Every man has to learn the points of compass again
> as often as he awakes, whether from sleep or
> any abstraction.
>
> —THOREAU, *Walden,* 'The Village'

To keep the compass circular
you stay awake, a phosphorescent
darkness that pegs its constellations.

There are no abstractions,
no knowing universe resets
its orbital rules, its polar

affirmations. I know sleep
would see me lap the poles,
eye the needle passing through;

extremities of light and temperature
strewn around to flock the hawk
and stall parrots like birds preying.

I can't devote time to learn
points of a compass again:
insomnia is assurance, a plan.

Settling House

Almost a year since we moved here
      and two years since we acquired
            the block—it's twice the house
               and twice the settling
               at this edge of total heat:
            what laws of contraction we touch
      with tightening shadows, each withdrawal
after the stretch has taken its edge of specification,

excitement at getting back into shape: but really,
      never precise, just an approximation
            that makes *give,* allows time
               its extractions: there
               is nothing perfectly
            elastic about a house, its unsettling
      and settling back into 'place'. The house
is contingent on location, its weather, the conditions

of its time: *en plein air* remonstrates what's seen
      without, what we feel as discomfort
            listening hard tucked up
               alone or together,
               all those messages
            of wakefulness, hours out in the heat,
      then coming in to gesture to night, to sleep,
to silence, the *almosts* since we moved here.

On the Great Red Storm

RED CLOUD

Pile-up on the hill crest made fold
thunderhead rising or plumes of smoke,
dead-heat day and southerly yet pall
cascading from the north, so smoke
smell and wind driving against approach,
then red cloud blackening sky, red cloud
eating all, too late to run we witness
and cry inside to see the world go
black-red inside the doomsday body,
sound of fury slashing trees to ground,
whiparound of sun's surfacing, solar
flares lashing out, rays cutting walls
that collapse on themselves. Left only
to senses and interludes of descriptive
awe, no subtleties of art or culture
to illustrate loss, though clues
might be had in cause, and survivors
allot reason or purpose to what they
drag their certainties out of, what
they fix as worth more than bodies
swept so quickly away, peeled back
like house roofs, the aged trees
that split and crash to the surface
that is but a suspension in liquid
changing qualities with red dust
that bloodies the storm, feeds death.

I.

Narrative version. Witness account.
Begs for story-teller, heroic rendering
to appease loss, or those tricks in point
of view, outlooking cloud travelled
down from red places, south, to unleash
or maybe just release contraindications.

2.

See discomfort in the sky and secure
loose objects about the block. See
the fulminating clouds nor' east.
Think of Kurosawa. An image outside
the register of this immediacy.
Not part of the tragedy.

3.

I call Tracy to come watch the culmination:
red–black counterpoint then mingling.

I fear fire without a whiff of smoke.
Anomaly that could leave no witness.

We agree it's not fire of the ground
but within the air, haemorrhaging sky.

Its approach is faster than we can run.
It lays waste to ideas of 'bearing down'.

We rush inside to young Tim who is
traumatised, and slam shut the door.

As the red cloud swallows the house whole
day blackens beyond needing torches:

it swallows all light redder black
by absorption. All light is eaten.

Trees scream and red dirt blasts
surface. Gratuitous. Scaramouche.

Aggregate. Amass. Strip bare. Polish.
Convene and multiply, twist and loss.

4.

Put into the past of conversation.

RED CLOUD AFTERMATH

I am draining redwater from the housetank
and in the scrimmage of leaves twirled
where tank stand meets the walls, vacuum
that formed when air tried to equalise—
a harsh brushing-up of foliage stripped
from whipped trees—I notice a delicate
golden cup, a nest of the finest inner
stems of wild oats, still flexible within
their outer sheaths of brittle stalk,
telescoped out by tiny pincer beaks,
calipers, wrapped around a lucid

planet of eggs that will core their lives,
but wrenched from its forked anchorage;
nest seething with ants amongst the bone
and down of hungry mouths fed
on storm, parents losing shape while
nest is dashed so oddly buoyant,
thrashed about, all of them, all of it.

Envoy

ON MELODECLAMATION

How has the stony earth
so effectively hidden the bones
of the people who came first?

Maybe the stones
are those bones
and we can't distinguish—

or won't—the sounds of native birds
accompanying our words,
fulfilling our wishes.